419 The Cyberscam Game

By

Jules Fonba

DEDICATION

To Danis, Krishna, Ntube, Jr. and Denzel

julesfonba@gmail.com/
https://twitter.com/julesfonba
www.julesfonba.itgo.com

Special thanks to:

Eugene Kingue

Gamsi Fabien

Alain Brice

Books by **Jules Fonba**

1) 419 Theft

2) Deep Witchcraft in the 419 Fraud

3) The Devil in a Cassock: Pedophilia wreck (*Inspired by a True Story*).

4) Last Wishes of a Dying Parent.

Note from the author.

I want to personally thank everyone who`ve been of vital aid to help me realized this project. The acquiring of information necessary to write this book has not been easy. Exposing an evil of this magnitude is not always welcomed by everyone; seen that, the level of infiltration is at all level of the society be it any name or offices you give.

When I took upon myself zeal to write this book and also it being my first book by then, the challenges were enormous. Many in this sphere actually feel wounded when the domain is talked about particularly in a massive exposure way like it`s done in this book.

My main goal was to expose and teach the people the danger involved mindless your country, race and educational background.

And wished all my readers to take it as a teaching book, even if you`ve never been duped online, you can still help someone in the future with the knowledge acquired here.

CONTENTS

1 INTRODUCTION

With the fast rate of cyber criminality today, one can deduce that, scamming has reached a zenith; where it can be equate to the Bill Gates constant updates of windows technology. In that ride, when he, Bill Gates, releases windows vista, or windows eight, scammers also come out with something state-of-the-art or more similar. Amusing right!

With the growth and success of cyber scamming popularly known as 419, in this new millennium, the ramifications have grown so profound than we can think of. With who, what, where, when, why and how being very imperative; particularly in terms of continent, country, region, culture, education, religion, gender and race. Deriving electronic forms and shapes to suit the target perpetrated; as each theory goes with a baptized name (*Nigerian Letter or "419", Phishing/Spoofing, Lotteries, job opportunity etc.*) Defining it genesis plus it history; if dim correctly. As these schemers particularly from the poor nations, often go with simplistic accosting, as their emails are usually embellished with intentional writing errors and naivety tag; luring the receiver into believing in a high class, economic or race superiority, which easily will lead to sweeping millions from this deal proposed. Neglecting clean the perpetrators professionalism and smartness in the act.

Some simply sacked and/or discontented ex-workers of strategy companies going back doors, and making good use of the loopholes, hereby giving birth to a scheme that will never be easy to hold back. In as much as, can be also political, economic or social discontentment of the system in place. For all these turn to be related in one way or the other.

The whole thing is very fast, too apprising and innovating in such a way that, we must constantly be on the alert. As no prepared police or security body can fight it on time. As it must always crush down victims mindless the definition you give about them, be it minister or lay man. And before preventive measures are taken to put on guard the public, which at times is not always an accomplishment, as to their unmasking, another scheme is already at hand and producing.

According to **Jamie Shea**, the Deputy Secretary General for Emerging Security Challenges, under NATO, a trillion dollar was lost in cyber criminality just in 2010 from a worldwide point of view, while interviewed in **Euronews Tv** channel (Land of cybercrime).

This book is going to be about discovering cyber scam, in a way you've never been told before. Lifting and shaking some vital points. In short, the best knowledge or wisdom you should have before ever doing any form of cyber business.

This flu that affects our cyberic world for time now has developed for aftermath, killings, frustrations, suicides, revenge, debts etc. Plaguing the planet for decades and due to man's poor alert system, wanton ego and quest to buy cheaply or get rich through shortcuts.

2 THE ORIGIN OF 419

This is the number one fraud game in the internet right now, with a popularity gone beyond all smashed hits one can gather, touching all borders of the world. It is deeply admitted to be the **West African Criminal Networks**. But many new questions arise nowadays like, are they, the only nationals practicing this Advance Fees Fraud (AFF)?

419 is that specified section of the **Nigerian Criminal Code** which bitterly condemns that act, that's, the penal code, under fraud and con artistry. A deception intentionally put at hand, in order to secure unlawful benefits, and wealth. Yet, the lucrative aspect of the games is so much so

that, many chance the risk, even to the height of government officials deeply conniving with the bandits.

419 involves credit card fraud, Nigerian letters, Disbursement/ pay out of money from wills scam, Work in a hotel abroad scam, Purchase of real estate scam, credit card fraud, Romance scam, Transfer of funds from over invoiced contracts scam, Phishing/Spoofing etc.

That's email exchanges, online phone calls, online payments, online chats, current information and free commercial ADS sites. Wearing the visage (identity) at times of true online companies i.e., **PayPal, eBay**, accosted with fictive sites or governments faces i.e. Nigeria bank, American green card lottery, to a perfect make believe to nourish.

This kind of cyber fraud was already in the corridors, before it explosive popularity now. It was widely known as the *"Spanish*

Prisoner Letter" during the 16th century. It involved postal mail, but by the early eighties, 419 saw it grand entry and takeover, to be the world`s most talk about, cyber scam, till today. Coming to the question posed in the first paragraph, this crime art is no longer an issue of West Africans or Africans of Nigerian Nationals based in one European nation or the other, true they might be the stars of it. But has become an *"An All Nation Business."*

It is only a personal desire then to a computer possession. Others become scammers, if been a victim and want to take revenge; the big difference here is that, some are more organized, well-disciplined and connected to state officials. Making it a solemn state affaire when least troubled.

3 EXPANDED METHODOLOGY

Cyber scam by pure definition is a scheme for making money via dishonesty, trick, subterfuge, hoax, tour de force, through the use of a computer and an internet line, alongside all it communication and exchange advantages.

Their main goal is to suck you into a lucrative pilfering; that is going to reshape the form of your life. Genuinely put in beneficial language to reassure and arrange the glittering of it success without any risk of involvement. Followed by a heavy pressure to get the business done and off to others. As it is always masterminded with theories of the eventual ending of the possibility if a firm grip isn't practiced. With well concocted lines like, **"the main man involved might quit or change his mind; it can be discovered if not act now; closing doors for this unique form of opportunity etc."**

You're spin to believe in this larceny, robbery, in a unique chance you've got amongst men. That`s, the spirit of God guided them to you, and eventually you're blessed and well loved by the Heavenly father.

Damn pitiful all these, as most are enticed into swallowing that, they've been picked out from the human community to share in multi-million dollar windfall gains, for being just who they are, and doing nothing.

Then, the other hot part for the people proposed to, is the amount or the percentage. This is a very crucial section in the email sent, as much care and approach is given to it, depending on the size of the deal or nature. Reasons pranksters prefer talking in percentages, leaving you calculate the figures. In the advent of this exciting payoff, you become anxious and want to know more; eventually you're lure by a desire to make a phone call or send a reply of the email etc. A debut to a clear downfall as the con artist is sure a victim is at hand, that would make him grow really fat.

As he's been given the first step, which is contacting him, the next move is harboring you in a notion of utmost confidentiality of the deal. In replicates like, **"he's personally taking risk, tax free advantage, if remain underground and in the fear of being discovered etc."** As a result, you accept to dance to his tune, after all, who likes paying taxes anyway. Once, this is done and well-sealed, he is sure to swim you to the end of the road.

As soon wrapped you into the first step,

the next move becomes the compactness of the swindle. He demands your postal address or/and sends you concrete documents via email attachments. Most often than not, they prefer the postal type to give in to more seriousness. These couriers are usually compacted with legal stamps, legal letterheads, and seals, with all authenticity; dressing the mind of the victim of it pure reality.

This pattern is very peculiar with Nigerian 419 scams, as they've made smashed successes and still making in their able multi-transfiguration of the plot visage in America, Europe and in potential Asian countries like Saudi Arabia, India, Singapore and Indonesia etc. Such forms bear the titles of general directors, managers etc.

The astonishing part of this stage is that, things begin to act in you as if you were hypnotized, because little reasoning and questioning is done to define ways and gestures; coupled with the fact that secrecy (*confidentiality*) has been implanted to the skull as a code. As you find yourself releasing your confidential information like fax number, telephone, account number, addresses, when demand solemnly to provide multiple signed and stamped blank company letterheads, invoices etc.

Then, arrive the role of the middlemen, as the signatories of the letters show it, and confirm by the vandal. All in a bit to concretize the norms of the contract, as requested by the bank, about to deal with; and if immediately accepted, cash will then flow into the victim's account. But little does the victim know this is the beginning of all his woes, in its actual definition. Upon reception of the required documents, as multiple requests arises from left to right, right to left, having the head and faces of taxes.

Calmly, you are then asked to transfer

money to recent encountered taxes, contract fees, attorney's fees, briberies of government officials and bank officials and so forth and so forth money drains out the pocket.

The victim might even be invited to the trickster's country to meet partners involved, before finishing touches of grand payment of the last advanced fees, often followed with minor traps like **"much is not over emphasis on certain immigration documents in my nation, particularly on legal travelling documents, that demands ability to be fully admitted to that country"** issues often taken very seriously at their immigration offices when reported or noticed. At times they are the one to even report you to start your trouble at the immigration office, why, because, they've got the connection too at that level. In fact, you're caught in their playground. The other step might be going forth with the staging of people in true government buildings to give symptoms of true approvals, alongside other attributes like expenses to welcome the board members that are going to preside to the final point of your deal.

But the night before the last deal, the victim is often invited to the scammers lodge, or to a place of partying, whereby a belly dance is organized to turn him on and on, to all forms of excitation, as welcome attitude; soaking the person to high space hospitality or say, frying him to his imminent calamity.

Brief, this being more or less an industry. As the victimization gets larger, so the dupers get more organized and sharp to the point. And if there is no possibility of going to the trespassers country, the target or victim is always referred to a neighboring nation for the deal to be enhanced there; depending on the ability to feel free, if the nation of the deal is too unfamiliar with usual nations of travel, of the victim with theory of having an expatriate operating in and around the corners. In some cases, say, acting like clearing houses for the monetary company dealing with.

And only God's knows how deep this kind of setup is, because most of these mischief-makers practicing these arts, and moving head high or fearlessly are always protected by someone in the high place, covering their asses, in times of hot crises. And at times the protection can even come directly from the presidency. Who ventures then? In this old adage *"You scratch my back, I scratch yours and everybody is fine"*.

Clear sense of why the sufferer (victim) might never recover his or her money or be satisfied to the fullest with the ways of investigating the problem. Raison d'être, **Ibrahim Lamorde** returned to the **EFCC** (*Nigerian Economic and Financial Crime Commission*) on 23 November 2011 after chairman **Farida Waziri** had been dismissed by President **Goodluck Jonathan**.

4 WHO IS A 419ER

It is that person or group of persons, known as 419er, of any reasoning age, who cannot be seen physically on first instance. That person that has the prankish ability to use a computer or the internet and bring out a well labeled system, to ripe you off, of what rightfully belongs to you, in the name of a deal that is going to make you everlasting rich. Or in the cheapest sale, you've ever encountered in the internet; over a product that you best know well, to be very expensive or rare.

Who has developed all diversify forms to come to you, as a seller, a businessman, an agent, a contractor, a philanthropist, an investor, a war victim, a widow, a heritor, lover etc. A perfect transformer; with all the force to gather his goal, and swell his pockets. This game plan, always having for target business tycoons, big companies, individuals, educational centers, charities, and governmental locations, has seems to pin a lot of destruction to the economy.

With exactitude, 419ers know where to get the contacts for their future preys, on websites that gives directories of potential partners or enterprises, newspapers with emails contacts, commercial libraries, trade journals etc.

And with the success they make from the scheme, turn at times, to re- invest into the swindle or/and go wider into immigration fraud, drug trafficking, stolen identity crime, credit cards theft; in order to have more power and reaching the target with all cleanness of make believe. Nigeria alone has the prestige of mails and emails as the third biggest exporting material in their economy. Particularly with their Facsimile machines faxing style, benefitting from web manipulations and going scot free, proving that, scamming has gone full crime organization and much money has been invested to enhance this bogus theory.

5 WHO IS FREE FROM 419

Honestly, nobody, nor matter your continent, country, region, culture, internal or external security, education, religion, gender and race; or, with who, what, where, when, why and how being the matter; you can still be a potential prey and the easiest of all.

This, because, 419 like the usual form of scam, is a big game of mental. That goes with the shuffling, the reshuffling and steaming of your desires. With heat of products to sell, banking emails to complain account overdue errors, promises and imaginary soon coming grotesque sums etc. That will forever marvel your life. After all, who will not like to add more zeros to his financial figures, or play the lord in his milieu?

At this point, the brainwashing is on the making, leading to the handing of all your basic information, on his dare demand (*photocopy of I.D, photocopy of pay slip, bank account number, address etc.*). Brief, all that will grant him credit and make you feel the authenticity of the business.

Once he succeeds in having a potential advanced fee or a multiple from you, the deal is done. The scenario has worked. Hearing from him becomes line of excuses or he just disappears from the circulation created with you. Or if, it's the number of your bank account number he has, (*foolishly given by you*); by the time you noticed it; your banker is already confirming to you, that, what you've labored all your life is gone for good.

Their evil has even gone long handed, as they even target charities with the holy desire to play the benevolent and mark their names in the list of philanthropist, claiming to give them money, but go again with their usual songs and styles of giving advance fees for this or that taxes to unleash the multi unseen dollars. Often on the make believe that, their past life had a lot of holes, or/and deadly sins and want to cleanse their conscience.

6 WHY IS 419 SUCH A HUGE PLANETARY SUCCESS

The spinning wind bliss of their reusiste (realization) lies in their ability to cotton on the mystery, **"Money Made the World"**. People only live for money and see it as their God, and would do anything to worth it. For all capitalist nations only breed on that; so do too, the functioning minds of its citizens. Power generator!

As the unmeasured ego for money here, goes with each individual; insofar, others are extremely encroached even in the visage of physical warnings. Overdosed spirits!

Education: People have surpassed the level

of learning to read and write only. People have cooked and frozen their inferiority complex, of seeing some class of human beings as lords to be adored and most respected. People have labored to go beyond their imaginations, and get things done for themselves. This, making it one of the greatest eras, in which the demerits are in their grip of determination and see their force of attraction work.

The level of illiteracy too, has greatly dropped, as compared to forty years ago. Particularly, when we look at it from the underdeveloped countries or nations like from Africa. Governments have invested a lot in educational means to fight intellectual ignorance and as a result, in many years of struggle, many elites have been born from all four angles of the block. This is seen with India, South Africa that has proven to be amongst the top emerging nations of our time.

Not forgetting that some modern human beings come out dotted with strange form of smartness and creativity in their system that when discovered in time, and well oriented to the goal pointed, becomes a phenomenon. Let just say **Hackers Boom.**

Paupers: The genuine exploitation of desperate humans, by taking advantage of their anguish, afflictions, torments, agonies and miseries, in promising heavenly solution for them. When we know, mankind is full of below standard souls. For example, a person in need of work, marriage, schooling, traveling, health care, assistance of any sort, for the betterment of their poor conditions.

And those in these conditions would give their last breathe, to see it happen; just to find themselves scrapped off, of their all, on a make believe theory. This is very monstrous, as we all know the poor and lowly, bear God's visage and mercy. And any touch on them, is a personal attack to him.

English language: The power of speaking English has also helped. Being the universal language for business and interaction, it has facilitated comprehension and breakthrough in this field. As three quarter of the world speaks English, and are Anglophones by their first or second language. And/or try to comprehend the language or force to do so, for the sake of marching to world's commercial and entertainment language.

Computer moved from luxury to a necessity: The advent of economic revolutions, with some countries, like the Chinese and Dubai; products of every grade have been made for accessibility to every citizen, of all standards of life in the world. Not forgetting second hand electronic products from the America and Europe; Opening bigger doors for scammers from poor nations to be more equipped, and effective. With the intelligence of transferring their overseas IP address to another country or nation based local server. Making traces and relay very difficult to track. Subsequently, recruiting more people to the hacker`s universe; as both scammers and hackers go good beer.

The doctrine of globalization: As all knowledgeable about the hoisted doctrine of globalization, that permits better interaction, so as to gain from the savoir and comprehension of the others; has fashioned it, the perfect global village. Transforming citizens of different nations, different interest to share in their technology, culture etc. thus, enticing less mefiance about others and opening wide ingress to deals, if really it's going to add more zeros to the coffers.

Easy business transactions: Still in the arrears of globalization, much has been invested in the technology of money transaction to ease up affaires. With the use of modern banking system, money can be send from any corner of the globe to you, or you to the other. Through wireless methods, clearing checks, internet banks like **PayPal, Visa, MasterCard, Western Union, MoneyGram, Swift Line**, have all helped to get scammers organized.

Intensive migration: The last eighty years has proven the greatest migration of our time. Particularly from all angles of the world, people have been so interested to repositioning as never before in the history of migration. This can best be understood from conventions or regroupings held by all citizens residing out of their countries, to maintain their strength and status quo, in terms of troubles of any sort. Mostly from less developed world to developed world, in search for greener pastures, education, work etc.

Opening doors to mastering the aborigines way of life, knowing their financial capacity, their economic strength, their mentality vis-à-vis money, in short all about their weaknesses. Permitting them to be aware on how to assault the prey, in the kind of language to use, the mentality to wear before reaching the goal.

Communication: This, has been broken down to the level of every ones reach. It is no more of a luxury or thing, which will go with heavy investments to acquire. With the discovery of wireless system i.e. **Wifi, optic fibers**, satellite interface has been made too easy for all. Especially developing states, longed been in political turmoil. Giving the cyber connivers roots to better profit, and make the industry a four star thing.

Medias: This is a very sharp point in the enhancing and the success of cyber scam. A lot of documentaries have exposed imperialism (*poor foreign polices*) and given heavy desire, envies and release of the height of some occidentals overzealous forms of life. The way they dilapidate their money, how they sit on mountains of wealth, waiting for God to give a price to come live in Heaven, whereas others are living hand to mouth, and below poverty level. Not only so, in their excesses, they spend more on pets than thinking of ways to survive man in his feeding calamity.

All these has help stimulated cyber scam, organized them, make them very determined as ever; believing, the best interpreters of the theory of golden law of attraction, that's why a plotter (419er) may never have gone out of his country or to big schools, but succeed in tuning you off your millions, with a make believe theory in your natal home.

Unregistered internet and cell phone lines: Inasmuch as, in the developed world, every subscription of any type, that's internet line, cell phone etc. is registered with your address or/and links of your address in which you can be traced from the central unit or from the national data base. But, while in some countries, this kind of federal law does not exist, mostly in West African nations; yet the grounds are still in high magnitude of loopholes in the process of prepaid system or stealing one's own, where high control is.

Faithless generation: As named by so many authentic men of God. The issue here is a drastic one, as man has greatly shifted himself to a total laissez-faire from the recommended ways of our lord, morals ethics and standard form of life. Making it hard for divine intervention in his dangerous moments, or even when comes, and signs of warnings is specified, does not still take note, in all seen and wanted is money and power.

Excessive use of mystical powers: In zero ability to pray or fear his creator for protection, man has opened the Pandora box for all sorts of evil possibilities to reach his milieu. Most uses powerful charms or forces, amassed from human parts concoctions, spiritual rites, incantations, black mass, and invocations of diabolic genius to turn issues to their favors. In credos, reaching the goals by any means necessitous, no matter who gets hurts. In this state, the scammer has no turning back. Who then denies that, they do sell out their souls too!

In this philosophy well understood by the 419ers; the least approach made and wealth spoken, the gate door is open, and a kingly dinner is served to the visitor from another dimension, who is going to change a life or/and make my bank account swell for good. Even at the edge of not having any money; obligatory measures are taken for fast borrowing mindless the interest rate.

7 A DEEP REGARD ON HOW MYSTICAL POWERS ARE USED

a)   **Charms:** We all know charms to be one of the oldest antiquities; one of the ancient devilish influenza in existence, since the creation of man to the biblical writings. We've seen and heard light fight and denounce charm as an instrument from Satan. Yet, this hasn't stopped it growth till this present day; where all have been proudly brought to notion as "De Rigueur" strictly required by the current fashion or the etiquette.

The risk zone here involves the world at large. Magic has been imported to many nations in the world as has been the case of

Europe and America the chief antiquity importers. Collecting all sort of fetish arts (*statues, mommies, objects of high spiritual believes and values*) from round the globe particularly from Africa and Asia.

These goes along with the theory, of each piece of arts carried out of it placed of derivation, has it strong fetish ties with it area of foundation and when moved from there, goes with it forces. Charms are of various dimensions and commands, alongside it fabrications mark (*can be from human parts, chameleon, strong formulas, idols or animals of rareness*). A high diabolic ability to captivate any spirit; at the voicing out of any rubbish, mindless the distance the victim just succumbs without any second thought. The only protection dynamism here against this, is prayers and exorcism.

b)   **Witch doctors**: The go-between; who talks, sleep, walk and go astral with the spirits. Knows and has it all to mirage the target from any part in the world. Their sanctuary always dressed in red loins and statues plus incents of all sorts as decorations. And he has the ability of an oracle, soothsayer, seer, clairvoyant or fortune-teller. He uses all the evidence that were foolishly given by the victim, at times, to cook him up to believe blindly, all that will be said and requested of him.

Nobody ever cheats him or play over his intelligence; and normally functions on percentage bases, as the treaty gives birth to seeable dollars. That's the more reason, why at certain point of the transaction, no matter what is enlighten to the victim, of the deal involve being a swindle, he will never believe till the concoctions reaches it gold, of bringing him to ruin. Individual at times under this spell, often go a-borrowing, borrowing from their banks, friends, relatives unconsciously. This is very dangerous and death can be the last result at times.

c) **Occultism**: This is the highest level of magic and the worst fetishism to be used on an individual. As all adepts are given the devilish authority to invoke, chat, live and commission spirits. Where they can monitor (*at times with crystal ball*) and kill at a distance with these powers. In another word, this is money rituals, the most dangerous diabolic spiritual arts, because every spirit invoked must get the task done or a boomerang.

Since the world is doing everything to its ability to sensitize people, pranksters are gathering themselves more to the adoration of Satan to reach their gold, by pledging for spirituality.

Being the lord of destruction, lies, pains, theft and death, Satan does gives more credit to this con game, and we know, all that goes with occultism, goes with human sacrifices of all esotericism. These sects attract mostly youths, students, big hearted women, men and highly placed personalities. Depicting only the advantages and hiding Satan turns for his dues.

Reasons Gurus are always fearless or heartless because they know their backings, as brotherhood stipulates the helping of a brother in any danger if in that position to help him or her. Not surprised if a phone call comes from the presidency to free the culprit.

Most will agree here, this sentence falls under top secret deals of extreme government, so watch out and pray so often, because, if you're in prayers, these things will never happen to you. This is a level beyond human manipulation and only the spirit of God can really refute it.

8 MOTIVATIONS

So many far-fish reasons go forth, as to why cyber scam is practiced. As said earlier with who, what, where, when, why and how being very important, particularly in terms of continent, country, region, culture, education, religion, gender and race. But one thing, married them all, that's the spirit of **Easy Money**. Now let see how their motivations goes in stages.

1. To Get Rich Or Die Trying

This goes with the saying, *"All Dreams for a Better Life Someday"*, and 419 becomes their mode to reach the dream **Eldorado.** This is by dragging the sufferer (*victim*) into believing in a juicy business, in a succulent contract, that's going to change his life now and forever. Thus, making them feel they can sack their boss with no pang of conscience. Within which, the target must be assured of it certainty, in fictitiousness.

In turning the machination true in asking the victim to produce his or her basic information; the name of bank, the address, the security number, the legal documents or one of them. In which it becomes the first success to cyber scammer and a monumental error for the victim. Thus, by such maneuvers; pave the gateway for the swindle.

Secondly, brain washing him to see himself like the initial contributor for the project by giving advance fees at times worth hundreds of thousands of dollars depending on the figures for the projects put forward. All in the name of make believe. Elevating him, go into trance, see floating bank notes.

2. To Make A Living

This is very common particularly with 419ers from average nations like *Nigeria, Cameroon, Ivory Coast, Benin, Jamaica, Ukraine* etc. Where there is monotonous economic strangulation; with little or no jobs available; frustrations and a blurred future being on the rendezvous.

3. To Be Respected

We all know the supremacy or sovereignty of money; it imposes some kind of force on the people, as it got no liable odor to tell it formal address. We live in a world where *"Money Made The World"* today. People just want to get their own piece of the cake and squander it ego force, why judge it genesis even if we know it. Let's respect him (*scammer*) and get our piece of the gold, after all, we are all tired of this poverty stricken life.

4. To Increase Seduction Power

The more economic potential you are, it's certain, popularity and fame is counted to your curriculum vitae. As both women and men will loiter and idle around you. Even the newly dismissed nun from the convent will like to get a piece of you. A deadly spirit that has attracted a lot of youths into the business.

5. To be seen as a Don (*lord*) in their milieu
This is the edge of power. The force to crackdown, the ability to harm or to change the course; kill you and bail self out if need be. The mightiness to impose fear and influence the local authority; where they will bow down to all your caprices as in the wheel of a **Don**.

6. Cultural, Regional and Educational Strength
This goes alongside the area of birth or growth, and the cultural practices around. In some corners, particular forms of dishonesty is very much accepted and regarded as a way of life. This is very common in poor countries or ghettos zones, where street begging, hustling, drug trade, child pedophilia;

human tracking and prostitution business is the order of the day. With the coming of cyber scamming, it all sounds like good business amongst the hideous others.

7. Easy Funds

To receive funds with little or no effort; where at times followed by zero necessity of codes or security number or even I.D cards to do the withdrawing. With what is needed is having the person's names and the trick is done.

8. Massive Greed of Foreigners

There is this wide notion that, foreigners particularly from the capitalistic world never give for nothing or if giving, that must be saddled with a secondary aim behind. The growth of modern imperialism, enhanced by some so-called giant nations attacking weaker states to take control of their wealth and government, profiting from their up rise and internal turmoil. By this philosophy of theirs which is theft and scam of another level, develops and nurses hatred and discontentment to fight back. Not to talk of constant world richest classification in terms of wealth, industrialization, dominations (G20, etc.); this alone make them feel it's perfect that they should scam them.

Hence, we must have our own share of the cake by like or by force, by fixing or by spoiling. And the only way to get them is by talking money, by making it look big, easy and cheap, as only money is in their minds. And today, it has proven very fruitful and rewarding.

419ers from developed world have a more complex and smoother way of doing their 419 thing. They scam everybody mindless their origin, but mostly their citizens or nations of the same economic power. They make use of actual problems to scam people online. That's through **Work At Home Schemes, Weight Loss Schemes, Fake Lottery Schemes, Computer Dispatch**

Schemes, Buy A Home Schemes etc.

9 WHERE AND HOW VICTIMS ARE CONTACTED

To where and how victims are contacted, goes with a lot of diversifications.

Many forms do exist and are invented daily, for example:

i)   *Referrals. (By friend, relation, neighbor, colleague, hater with vital clues to the person).*

ii) *SMS (Short Message Service) through mass systems like WASPS etc.*

iii)   *Chat rooms offered by free dating sites.*

iv) Magazine based on business and economy updates. v) Untraceable Phone lines.

vi) Fax.

vii) Courier/post/mail.

viii) Internet call line (VOIP).
ix) Invitations to scammer's nation.

x) Computer program called BOTS.

10 WAYS OF ACTIVATING THESE SCHEMES

There are two ways of activating this scheme in the internet. First one, is what we will name as, **The- Victim- To- The-Scammer** and the second and most popular one, is **The-Scammer-To-The-Victim.**

i)   The victim to the scammer (*Me To You*)

This form of 419 is usually provoked by a **Soon-To-Be-Prey**. What do we mean by this, this is when a person develops the interest to buy a thing from the internet, be it of any nature, a pet, a house, an object of high valor. Consults a website with free ADS display and then finds himself in claws of a well sharpen scammer.

Playing the perfect business tycoon and concocted. In this mood, most often than not, the buyer has little or no prudence it can be a scammer. And usually with very cheap amount on the discursion, ticking little suspicion. As all the information he ask about you, comes out without any second thought that it might be cyber scam.

ii)   The scammer to the victim (*You To Me*)
This is the one En vogue, and most ravaging form of 419 fraud. For as long as, people have never had the decency to ask themselves, why they have been enticed into believing they have been singled out from the populace to share in multi-million dollar windfall profits for doing totally nothing, 419ers will continue to ride in flying horses and dress in robes of prince and kings. Here as usual, the con artist plays a proper transformer, that's, **a contractor, buyer, seller, agent,**

philanthropist, clergy, church, and widow etc. to reach a victim. Premiered with the confidential nature of the transaction emphasized and in almost every case around is a sense of urgency. Leading to the revealing of all confidentialities about you and your family and in each fees requested for processing the transaction pertaining to be the last required.

11 FREQUENT DISPUTES BETWEEN 419ERS AND HOW THEY SETTLE THEM

A) Frequent Disputes

Most of these problems arise from group scamming, where much labor, money, and strategy is invested. For a single scammer, is far from having any scratch with a fellow brother scammer. The main things that causes trouble between scammers are betrayal, blackmail, percentage problems, jealousy and set ups.

i) Betrayal

This can come in the form of a threat from the rival group, by keeping captive, one of the members when a very lucrative deal is at hand. Or as a pressure from the police, to act the inner man to label out the major plans, and under threats of imprisonment, of sentence reduction, in the court of law due to their co-operation. Thereby, forcing information out that can lead to the compromising of the deal.

The betrayal can still come in a form of revenge amongst discontented member or members and prefer to destroy all, even at their entire detriment.

ii)   Blackmail
In every dominion of any brand, we all know people to blackmail, coerce, and extort to keep to their status or impose them to standard. Again, these things only work with two or more individuals framing together.

From telling effect, blackmailing only ride, when I know your innermost acts or/and much more about your skeletons. Always a bad portray for the future of the assemblage. It can be one member having an affair with another member's wife, sister, child, relations etc. which goes contrary to the laws and values of the group. One of them may use this knowledge to extort money or influence the other, on things not very much appropriate, making it a very pertinent problem for him.

iii) Percentage disagreements

We know the world is jam-packed with people whom we can never trust or have faith in, when it comes to coinage. Even in the face of stated percentages to be share hereafter the pact, will always find ways to hoax things at the end.

As a result, 419ers always suffer from setbacks of double-crossing either from the complicity of one or two members to dupe the others or one person to sweep the whole clan. Others do it and remain on the spotlight, knowing there are untouchable, because of their past criminal records over dealing with people who dare oppose their actions.

Specifically in skyscraping lucrative deals proved successful. He sees these as an opportunity to become mightily rich and retire from the business in a faraway country, state or city. In transferring all their labor to his personal account, after all, it`s a game of dishonesty.

iv) Jealousy

This is always a very dangerous weapon in the criminality world; being bodies that only enrich themselves at the detriment of genuine people dishonesty is bound to reign. Always, they`re filled with all sorts of mal-resentments and evil concocted minds; commencing with envies, setups to do away with the prospering neighbor. At times, the cleansing can be done without the direct notion of the group, that's where the security tendencies of the group becomes very vital, as all is put to action to know where the bug is shooting from. And woe be tide you the culprit, when discovered.

B) How They Settle Their Scores

Most of their disputes are settled in many ways depending the area where found and the tendencies of cyber scamming there. That's amicably, by compensations or by violence.

i) Amicably

A meeting is held with the two bodies. By a leader of a more renounced 419 league, to bring a truce and avoid any bloodshed. Usually followed by a penalty, where all obey without any argument. Or to the faulty person, who caused the problems. Another option can be the faulty one going to meet the baffled 419er, for a peaceful agreement and settling their differences without any need for gunshots or repose setups. Most often than not, this is very rare, because no one will forgive so soon, a person who dares him with a murderous back stabbing intentions. Knowing very well that, they are all far from being Saints, as they all live and practice evil; no way for such peace, for once attempted, for sure, will soon begin again. Protecting your back, they all say as they fire back the enemy.

ii)   Compensation

Usually by compensating the other for the offence done, helps to calm down tension, and tilt them more for the future. This can be in the form of money, asset or a possible option and percentage in the con deal at hand. As more, should be gained ahead rather than persisting on something, which will only plunge them heavily to hate and possible bloody confrontations. After all, they belong to one Republic, and share the same 419 citizenship.

iii)   Violence

This is the most reputed form of settling their woes. Can you just count how many times when you switch on your television set, and get wind of the breaking news, of gun shots, between rival gangs, in your neighborhood, city or state? Plenty right.

But just that in this milieu, there is always a lot of usage of hired killers to do the eradications. It can be an operation car bomb, tripwire at the residence, a killing of a family member through kidnap, filing of evidence to the police of your dirty businesses or gunshots with snipers tact, etc. But for our African scammers to solve such embarrassment, many have opted for the mystical strength of *Odeishi*; the mystical bulletproof magic which permit them not to die by gunshot.

12 HOW THEY ARE ORGANIZED

To have an extensive comprehension, let's see how they are regrouped:

1) Single 419ers
This form concerns any individual who does this dishonest scheme through individual means. Using own tools and intelligence to make the target fall. Smarty! This trickster is acquainted to all powerful transformation, and by all configurations needed. He can spend even twenty hours daily in front of the computer, in none, so good in the usage of **BOTS** software then him. Prevalently known in Nigeria as the **Yahoo Boys**, accepting to be jailed-up in cyber cafés till morn, in order to slickly boom the industry and make victims'

rain.

2) Duo 419ers

Here is the company of two men or two women or a duo of a man and woman and in some cases, a wife and a husband or lovers. One is always specialized in something that the other cannot do perfectly or at all. So they sum up to make better halves. And the smooth running of the scheme is assured for seduction, lies, theft etc.

3) Hired 419ers

Like a hired gun, so too, scammers are hired to scam someone online, with all basic information given by the client, at times an ex and discontented employee; a jealous friend or relation that has all the clues to harm.

It can also be a person who has worked in strategic corners of a company or government offices, that has all the access to sensitive domains, pension codes, security numbers etc. and to remain clean, prefers to hire cyber fraudster to hack the system. Like the old adage says, *"Evil Never Comes from So Far"*.

4) Family 419ers

A family issue where embedded brothers and sisters, with parents too, at times as accomplices, each having a dynamic role to play. In who answers the phone calls with multiple voices, replies the email, hacks and does the financial backings and the withdrawal from the money agency. This is not very common in the scamming industry.

5) Quarter 419ers

This involves the harden delinquents of the neighborhood, spreading fear and seducing respect. With never an attempt from anyone to sell them out to the police, or get yourself and your family in danger. Where everybody knows everybody and will trace the least itch.

6) Students of colleges and universities

These are one of the most dangerous

scamming groups; this is because they see scamming like a way to gain high opinion, veneration, esteem and deference amongst their friends. And will do it again and again mindless the deadly risk and to maintain their status and their life trench.

The notorious campus scammers always behave like members of an occult group, as they move together; hold meetings at strange hours of the night, in their massy attitude of proper Dons. A tick to race eye brows. For, universities has always been the cradle of initiation to major and minor sects that reign the world today like the popularly known **New Age Sect**.

7) Nomads or Inter region 419ers

Also known as *travelers, wanderer, itinerants, rovers or zonal cyber scammers;* they move from one cyber café to the other, in different regions or states. Each prey begotten, one sector or town is chosen, with a specific internet center for the scheme, and as immediately done with the victim, they change county (region). In this blight, you will never know their earthly position or their exact IP (*Internet Protocol*).

This is to dissimulate the idea of one address spot, and to avoid any form of tracker from the internal or the external world. They also practice this form of scamming to quit away from the local police, if already in the list of wanted or most sought after, in the country.

8) Intellectual group 419ers

They`re considered as gentlemen of zero-suspicion; where also regarded as full time businessmen; to know and understand more of what is said in this sector, watch the movie *'Ocean Eleven', 'Ocean Twelve',' Ocean Thirteen'*. The cleanest and most dressed business guys in town. Who don't go to hidings at times, but comes out plain, with all documents and visibilities, that shows the means and possibilities to do business, whereas, inwardly fake, masked with ample stratagem to endure you to error to their own advantage.

Whereby, each member is a proper dude to his con specialization; very disciplined and respectful to instructions of their con leader, the brain box, the Einstein, often loaded with heavy criminal past to keep the state officials on the watch.

9) The untouchable Gurus

This is the big brother level swindling, where much money is involved, with multiple six zeros amount concern. They, gaining approach security, assurance and backings, right from top government officials; literally from the look of things making it a state affaire when on their way. In their (*government officials*) own percentage pressed, as the deal proves a success.

That's why scamming will always involve the catching of the minor ones, and the big fishes continuing to reign in that wonder of dishonesty scheme. It is the highest network of scamming, where all has it locale and well put to order. With little or no fright in their endeavors, true state scammers.

Here individuals are recruited under the notice of high particular talents to dupe and to pass through, in their dishonest field of expertise, at times with your like or dislike meaningless to them. Particularly those who've worked in high strategic posts of their country, and having broad notions about the persons or the companies they are going to tamper with.

In most cases, the organization can go as far as getting out a harden criminal from prison to get a particular job done, if dim necessary, just to reach their gold. That's where the role of government officials becomes vital, discrete and real.

To put an end to this kind of organization, it always demand the alteration of government delegates, or a coup d'état and, as soon as, it is dissolved, so fast does it comes back to fabrication. Because, it is a very hot money-spinning business, as sufferers are always there to make fall dollars and millions of it.

13 DISCRIMINATE AND INDISCRIMINATE SCAMMERS

1) **Discriminate scammers**: At this junction, we breathe the congregation of scammers that have a particular steer as their objective. That's, their zone of preference can only be breezed according to their strong feelings; can be loaded sectors like the West, and the Arab world or only Europe and America. Others might choose everybody apart their nationals.

2) **Indiscriminate scammers:** These guys are the cruelest and most diabolic, who are always on the run and lonely. The most heartless in the industry, in every creature a potential prey, be it a neighbor, a friend, a tribes person, a relative, a fellow citizen or a foreigner , all of them are the same in front of him.

Those practicing this form are always the first to die strangely in the game, and nobody borders enough, because in most minds and much more near to him, they are always buried before their true funeral.

For home is home and anybody who tampers with its natural numbs, always come to the fast answering of it. In no sweet curse like direct from home.

Where we say, *"Scamming Eat Its Own Child"*

14 A GRAPHIC REGARD OF INITIALIZATION INTO CYBER SCAMMING

Like a newly bought computer that needs installations, so is the brain of he, who wants to become, a cyber-scammer or a 419 in general. He needs to be configured to the arts, particularly with handling of the merits and the demerits. Hoping at the end to win the valor of "THE BORN TO DO IT TYPE."

419 THE CYBERSCAM GAME

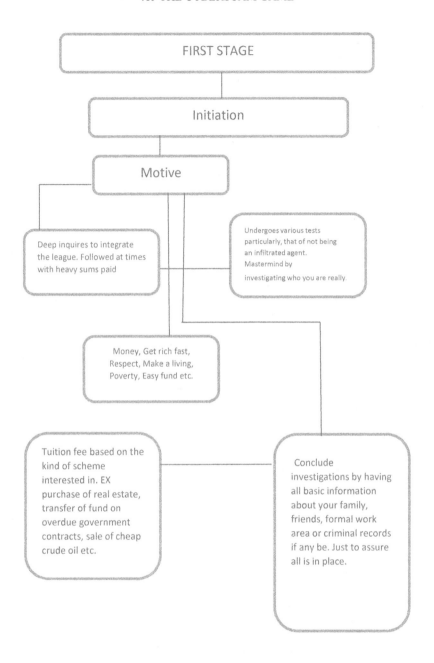

FIRST STAGE

Initiation

Motive

Deep inquires to integrate the league. Followed at times with heavy sums paid

Undergoes various tests particularly, that of not being an infiltrated agent. Mastermind by investigating who you are really.

Money, Get rich fast, Respect, Make a living, Poverty, Easy fund etc.

Tuition fee based on the kind of scheme interested in. EX purchase of real estate, transfer of fund on overdue government contracts, sale of cheap crude oil etc.

Conclude investigations by having all basic information about your family, friends, formal work area or criminal records if any be. Just to assure all is in place.

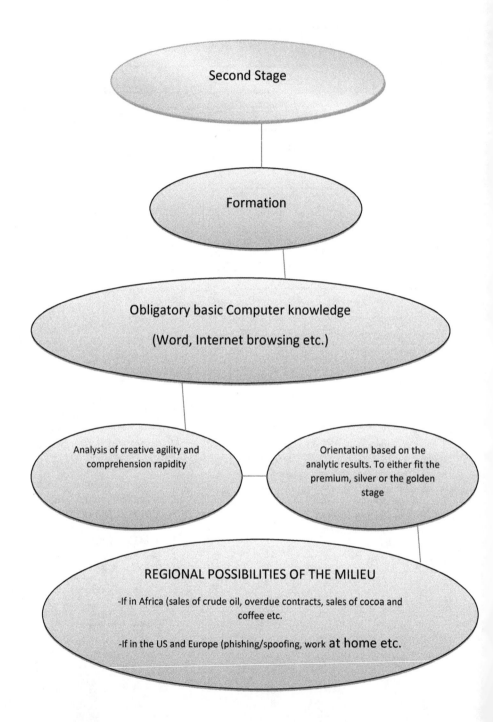

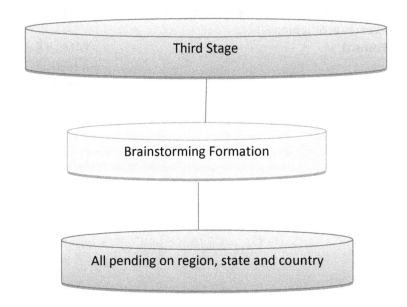

ASIA & MIDDLE EAST	EUROPE & AMERICA	AFRICA
TECHNOLOGIES (Computer & high tech accessories)	ASSETS & WEALTH (Get rich fast pandemic etc.)	MINERAL RESOURCES (Gold, Blood diamonds etc.)
INVESTORS (Petroleum companies, oil refineries owners, Governments)	INVESTORS (Petrol companies, Government officials etc.)	POLITICAL INSTABILITY (Civil war & Genocides etc.)
TRAVEL, STAY AND WORK ABROAD (Building and Modernization companies, Hotel,	NGOS-Nongovernmental organizations (Travel, Stay & work abroad: hotels,	DISEASES (HIV Aids, Malaria etc.) POVERTY (Lack of means,

Building & Construction expertise, Shipping & Transit)	babysitting, military enrollment etc.)	Plead for charity etc.) FAMILIES & KINGDOMS (Heritage & families, Bribery & Corruption etc.)

15 FORMS OF ADVANCE FEES

There are two types of advance (**Up-Front**) fee plot. The **Single Advance Fee Scheme** of the small deals is where the prey is sucked once and for all.

The **Multiple Advance Fees Scheme**, is where, the prey can find himself with almost a million dollar donation or more. This, bit by bit as reasons lay out.

i) The Single Advance Fee Scheme
This kind of con artistry involving onetime fee is mostly common with plots concerning work online jobs, rent a house for holidays online, buy pets online, buy a product online,

refund overdue money or a tool etc. It's always consisted of very small amounts.

ii) The Multiple Advance Fees Scheme

It's the grand style of the fraud game; classified as the golden level in the 419 industry. Most often enhanced by a team of well-trained scammers, with an unimaginable force of attraction in their determination, each with a potential criminal record. Alongside with a first rated computer genius, who can hack any system, particularly in the banking system.

Here, there is always a need for urgency, many forged official documents, confidentiality emphasized, and online phone calls, with numbers always beginning with 006, 007, 008, 00228 and multiple voice trafficking accent ability etc. on their menu. Coupled with the proposal of money from **Will Hunted, Cheap Crude Oil Sales, Transfer Of Millions From One Zone Of Deposit To Another**, bla bla bla. With each deal going with taxation advance fee, stamps advance fee, bribery advance fee, displacement advance fee, and so on and so forth. Alongside having taken all vital documents and information of yours, on pretext, that's the procedure. Finally ending in the cyclone of nothing, and ruin for the prey, and a fulltime victory for the scammer or 419ers.

16 SAMPLES OF ADVANCE FEES

At this height, there's no doubt that, you've become the backbone for the agreement, as any fees or taxes that threatens the moving of supposed funds, becomes your primordial concern.

In going through till the end, or become the loser of a treaty that would have changed your life and those around you. Ink marked with languages like, *"Is Going To Be Fine, It Is The Last Of The Agenda, That We Are Done With It At Last"*, but to the turn of the next page, another unexpected requested fee comes in again, in form of a crucial twist, more shaking than the other. And these goes on for weeks and months, the person in the form of victim becomes very certain that he or she will never see all the economy vested to the so-called **Transfer Fund Deal.**

Making it the lucrative objective for the 419er involved. As the scam has been a full success and he can repose himself or travel from one nation to the other, or to the country of the person scammed. Using letterheads and legal documents given by the victim to him to acquire a visa. It always very pitiable to see how people of high intellect and powerful command, are swindle to this con game by lads who are just merely smart and uncultured to manners. Some samples are

1. *Contract fees.*

2. *Export or insurance fees (helping money safely to foreign bank accounts).*

3. Attorney or lawyers' fees.

4. Transaction fees.

5. Demurrage, storage or release fees by a Security Company.

6. Communications fees.

7. Licensing or registration fees.

8. Advance fees or up-front fee.

9. Transfer taxes, performance bonds.

10. An anti-terrorist certificate fees.

11. Mandamus fees.

12. Drug Free Certificate fees.

13. Bribery fee, Etc.........

17 WHERE AND WHY SCAMMERS CHOOSE TO RESIDE

The factors influencing where and why cyber scammers operate their schemes can be broken down into structural (*urbanization*) development, technology development, security development. Schooling reasons, national and international reasons.

1. Urbanization reasons: It is very obvious that, anywhere there is a high urban development; all sorts of activities will be at their reach; that`s the good, the bad and the ugly. Most 419ers reside there for easy accessibility. And still, particularly, to be near international banks, money exchange agencies, co-operatives, airports, embassies etc.

2. Technology reasons: Where technology is available, that's, internet connection and stable one, and online phone calls with masked numbers; the reasons are good enough to be there, because cyber scamming goes alongside with high internet line stability. Mostly applied with 419ers from less develop world; unlike in developed world internet is the easy accessibility.

3. Security reasons: This is the business has reached a point where, serious measures have been taken by various governments and international bodies to fight it, particularly countries like America, which suffers a great deal from it; of almost a trillion million dollars annually dashes to the pockets of 419ers worldwide. Cyber scammers with all their accessories, of laptops and a good connectivity, prefers moving from one region to another, for fear of being caught; mostly those with the **Single-Scammer-Type** or those with little financial backings to protect their ass. Other reason as compare to why they move from place to place is to escape being tracked down, through a permanent IP usage and/or using software that dissimulate their IP or in one single region. That's from one cyber to another. This helps to destabilize investigators using any form of medium to grip them.

4. Schooling reasons: Being a business of easiness and fame. Most coming generations are deeply seduced by these structure; chiefly, university students. Many get involved in this ruse, to make fast money, to impress and get respected. Principally from nations where there is impoverishment, high unemployment rate, and landing into this business, is already preparing you for lucrative future career.

5. Godfather reasons: The Godfather being the prime mover and ever the ringleader, be still the one to resource to, shelter to, when things turn out of hand. He has all the main contacts, both from other 419 gurus, and also of government officials to always make use of begotten contacts within his years mal practices. As in this realm, you can be obliged to be indebted forever to a person; be you a clean man or not. For long as you've been saved from the lion's darn in the past, you must bend. Most of which is common with single scammers, or growing group, making Godfathers fulltime commission earners.

6. National reasons: This orbit is most concern with the Gurus, having lots of means and connections with governmental officials in the acting, playing the Godfather, in what is known as **Organized Cyber Crime**. They are found everywhere needs-be to enhance the scheme, because they got the means and aim the bigger means.

This is known to be found in **Contractors Scam Scheme**, where they clear the bush head high. In languages like **"In Oil**

Refinery There, In That Zone, We Run It, And Headquarter Here, In The Main City, Our Base". With accomplices scattered all round the nation or even internationally, claiming to be a clearing house for the presume bank dealing with just to magnify the scam.

This fraud is normally quite sophisticated and extremely well executed. Main objective, bring the prey to the source and set a whole scene of fake government officials, in offices of legitimate government buildings with true government letterheads and stamps on the menu. Clear proves someone within the government is aiding the guys out for a better percentage.

18 HOW THEY SPEND THEIR MONEY

It is very funny but must be acknowledged that, the way 419ers use or squander their dishonestly begotten money does not necessary reflect smartness of the way acquired. Very few use theirs wisely, and for those who do, nearly three quarter of their investments do not carry their names. It is either under the name of their child, mother, sister, brother or a Hench person of true trust. As we fight them, so too, do they fight money laundry.

a) **Assets.** At least three quarter of 419ers do invest in assets; buying plots plus houses here and there. In which later set for renting and reselling after revitalization. Depending on the worth holding at hand. As early mentioned, most of their assets don't usually carry their personal names, for fear of the future. Or if want to take the risk, then share the ownership with another person; the possibility of backstabbing becomes practically impossible.

b)   Banks. A scammer can have more than twenty bank accounts both home and abroad. The reasons are very simple. This is to avoid any raise for alarm. To make it again more concrete, the account becomes a joint one with someone of their choice and trust, where no money is taken without the knowledge of the other.

When he succeeds in duping four million dollars for example, the better way to avoid questioning is tallying them in the twenty accounts. Or go straight to an anonymous account abroad. Maybe to countries like Singapore that never questions the where forth of a client worth, but welcomes all.

c) Business. With the first money begotten, usually little business is raised up to do cover-up as a businessman. This can be a restaurant, bar, dressing shop, or a multiple ownership. At times, these corners' backyards do serve as their pentagon, to draft their future stratagem.

It should be noted, this guys are always the first to be regular in their taxes, and with all legal documents requested by the government for any form of local business.

d)   Parties. For those somehow anew into the business, the best and the most preferred ways to spend their money is by throwing their weight about. In organizing or/and going to sumptuous parties, where they sit on the highest tables, and command the most expensive liquors. By so doing, they single themselves out in their waste abilities; dressed in very high authority and in the most expensive garments in the market. Drowned by the most beautiful women in the spot, often prompt to throw money around, and witness them scramble over it; as escorted by praise singers if common in their regions. With one thing in their minds, **"There Is Still Much Money To Be Gotten In The Near Future."**

e)   Gambling. Like the old fashioned scamming, of duping your prey physically, the computer has only helped, put men behind the curtain. But not change their harden hobbies.

As the devil gives you so easily with the right hand, so too, he finds another way to help you dilapidates fast and go back again to immediate search with the left hand, which at times, can be your last humanly attempt, because you could get killed. And a good example of this form of wastage goes to the love of betting, gambling, casinos or anywhere or on anything that defines it.

f) Family. Obviously, they spend their money with their family, by offering a comfortable life to their spouse and children, in a total modern family of the hearsay. The wife wears all the latest marks she desires, jewelries etc. So too, the children, go to very expensive schools, accosted by a well-trained driver and bodyguard, if need be.

In most cases, they are the first to have all the latest electronic accessories in the market; with holidays here and there, both home and abroad; in a nutshell, a pure luxurious life at their base. In some cases, like in very poor areas, these guys, do settle some of their family members, into doing a business, buying a house, whatever the need be.

Yet, a lot of precaution is taken by some wise ones, by never letting any family member join their dirty business. For them, their (*scammers*) end can always be anytime. And will prefer going alone, than leave a relation to that game of risk. In just like the cocaine business, when you never know which one might be your last trip or deal.

g) Security. Nearly all 419ers do think of their security at least once a day. This is because, amongst them, you might never know, who will stab you, or sell you up to the cop, or the enemy around. You might never know when a possible repose might befall you. So, much is invested in security. They benefit from four types of security, the bodyguards security, electronic security, police security and lastly, spiritual security.

1) Bodyguard security.

These guys are either hired from local security firms to be in and around them 24/7. Or guys recruited from praises of their muscles, and their formal *banditism* echoes. What is usually referred to as the able men or watchdogs assuring total confidence for the space.

2) Electronic security.

This form of security is mostly found in their lodgings or buildings. They invest in high tech security cameras, of exposed and unexposed type, infra-red devices and silent alarms to alert when in or out of their houses. A kind of James Bond gargets of security where there zero tolerance for silly errors.

3) Police security.

This is unbelievable but very true. This is the method that most organized crime bodies in the world have been using for decades. Usually using threats or renting services of corrupt cops yearning to make more money mindless spitting on their sermon and batches. They main task is to act as informants who observe and leak sensitive information. He plays the guardian angel for the criminal and in return, serious commissions are paid to his offshore bank

419 THE CYBERSCAM GAME

statements or in cash. Others do it out of pressure, fearing the killing of their family member etc. But this option is very rare.

One of the reasons, the police force is known to be one of the most corrupt bodies in the planet earth as regarded by many wise brains.

4 Spiritual security.

This is the topmost form of security. It goes with fetish practices and deepest methods of Satanism; a pure black magic philosophy that's having a lot of faces to tackle with like the witchdoctor and vampire pastors.

This is because no true man of God will ever condole or endorse such practices, and give God's blessing to it. Most often, these protections goes with adepts from the dark institution, or serving the dark world. And heavy sums of money are often involved;

followed by good percentages, when succeed. The 419er can be given a talisman, a ring, beads, statue, bangle, incents to burn, or powerful charms made from human parts, to protect first then seduce and lastly, reach their goals with little or no effort. Or always consult the warlock before any important move, making it very hard at times for police, or any anti-cybercrime body to pick them up.

Being in a faithless generation, most of these things are bound to be a success when applied on the prey. Reasons, most never really understand, how they got themselves rubbed into this mud.

For any human being fervently into prayers, is always guarded by God's spirit. At times, he (God) might be talking to you in other forms, of the error you're about to make, but when the love for money, and the will to get rich quick overtakes; the next thing is loses and cries.

19 THE ADVANTAGES AND DISADVANTAGES OF CYBER SCAM

Advantages

Economic advantages: Under this point, 419ers are known to be very heavy consumers, devourers and lovers of fashions and high-tech entertainment devices, doing it, either in the smart way or usual way. They love investments in real estates and quick money businesses like casinos, showbiz with the use of a front man bearing the riches.

Some keep their monies in the banks, both home and abroad, that produces heavy interest as the banks turn affaires with it, hereby increasing in the economic growth of their world. Access to travel abroad becomes very easy, as all indicates business deal with a legal company or potential person abroad, with used of all legal documents given by the prey.

Political advantages: The worldwide desire for cyberic theft annihilation has let to many national talks, conventions and signing of many treaties allowing bodies fighting this domain to exist in their country. A good and true visible organization of this caliber is the *Interpol* found in nearly all the countries round the globe and dealing in more than one issue. With their number one priority being, tracking international criminals; has proven very efficient in information tapping.

America, graded as one of the highest countries victim of 419 theft, has united two of it forces, *the Secret Service*, under its mandate to protect US monetary system, that's it financial and currency institution to work hand in hand with their *department of commerce*, alongside with members of Nigeria EFCC (*Economic and Financial Crime Commission*) to fight this flu since the mid 90's. Thereby, increasing political stability with nations ready to co-operate and carry operations, at times to some vital assistance if a nation having economic problems.

Modern Social And Moral advantages: The modern society has become, the one that many people don't question too much the whereabouts of someone's wealth and if there are questionings, it comes from cops and only in case of a problem. Instead, humans enjoy and admire their lives and/or the sudden flow of wealth in their lives. Seeing it like a real updated social and moral advantage, this is because they are given the same honor and respect at times even with a lot of fear of person incorporated. This is mostly seen in developing countries, like Nigeria, Cameroon, and Benin, where a lot of rites and patronization is done.

Electronic advantages: The love of computer manipulation has risen so high; amid all, it is no longer seen like a luxury but a necessity of modern existence. Hence, many have understood that, what can be begotten from using it, is far much important than just having it. *The power of a well labeled scheme that hatches dollars.* Hereby, boosting the computer exploration deeper, as the fraudulent money begotten can give much ways. Mostly, in the under developed world and with ascension of the Chinese economy, accessibility has become easy for the rich and the poor. Not sparing out overnight releasing of software potentially supporting (**Chat rooms, bulk SMS, Webcams etc.**)

Educational advantages: Every person interested in cyber scam business must always be evaluated educationally before dashing into the industry; and the work of a real mentor is to begin from there. From the epicenter, only true learned guys, with visionary, smart and creative tendencies will really make it in the industry. In this blight, education becomes indispensable and he who wants to get in, must go to school to a level of diploma, reasons most of the biggest names in the scamming history, go with good educational background, for instance *Bernie Madoff* known as one of the greatest swindlers of our century.

Disadvantages

Economic disadvantages: Unlike the advantages outlined, 419 fraud is a tool that has helped empty the pockets of many big and minor businesses round the globe.

It has ruined many savings of a life time. Most of them (fraudsters) that do invest in businesses of other diversification go with the faith of hot gains and with cheaper sales to free out the goods immediately, something that in the usual and legal trade, will not be the same. Frustrating the economic logically and forcing the legal merchant to fast and uncalculated debts.

Like the Mafia community whereby only 0.2percent of their wealth is recuperated, some potential scammers too, have made their money a well-protected wealth, and must see it grow in figures or consume it, before apprehension by lawmakers.

According to the American secret service, late 90's saw the filing of complaints ranging from about 14,000 complaints a month, from its citizens pertaining to reception of these fraudulent emails or mails. And this is expected to have tripled ten years after with more nations being as ever involved thus making it a huge blow to the economy of most minor sector of trade, as some refuse to come out to declare their losses of fear of embarrassment and bad press for their companies.

Political disadvantages: Despite the agreements made to work hand-in-hand between governments, these things go alongside with a lot of threat, mal-resentments and tension from the victim nations, as murder cases are always recorded in this cruel game. It is believed that almost 84 billion dollars has been loss to scamming since 1980's to present date with use of 419 schemes worldwide. This is no good news for bilateral relationship.

As it makes diplomacy an outward type, and increases a lot of mefiance (*care*) in affaires provoking those spirits. Furthermore, it has been recorded that, most of these schemers are protected at times or individuals involved, do have very strong ties with potential members of their government; by consequence, making a mockery of the agreement on transparencies made by both parties to join forces fight the con game. This alone goes forth with pure declarations of its ramifications, being more profound as we expect. By diplomatic ties, things are forced to go on the strain, when tampered on.

Social and moral disadvantages: Society has reached its peak of moral decadence, in which we have the supporters of all the pros, and all the cons, of the contemporary age. People tend to reason more to the direct advantage the hideous comportments brings to them, rather than the effect in terms of manners for the betterment of the society.

As a result many minor minds have grown up with the feeling and certainty, of some immoral acts cultivated to be very much enchanted and acclaimed in their milieu. This is a very clear factor about 419 fraud as lies, dishonesty, double jeopardy, blackmail and gangsterism has become the order. Most often than not, it takes God's grace for a soul in that kind of milieu to be sensitized up and be save, for he is constantly reminded that what he is doing is good, and must always be that way and worth dying for.

Electronic disadvantages: Rather than electronic easing up life for man, it has been transformed into a perfect weapon to swindle, that's has helped cause many forms of instabilities. In the biggest computer and cyber treat called hacking. With adepts flowing in, every day, every hour, from the four corners of the world.

Money being the sole train admired by all, hence the zeal of making the world a better spot has fast died off; the collectiveness or the betterment for the entire human good has faded in the human soul. As every percentage of human good has been converted or overtaken by the scam corner of man. Many boosting of their scam deeds without fear again as their milieu sees it as normal and wish were in their shoes.

Educational disadvantages: Same too like the electronic disadvantage; knowledge or brain force that could have been used for the safety of humanity, creativity or for the amelioration of countries economy is tilted to false use. Many are brainwashed into easiness, which sooner grades them like international criminals, leading to imprisonment and premature death.

As parents and educational assistance co-operations spend a lot of money to educate, magnify and expect children to come out as refined human beings to lift the family name high rather dragging it on the mud.

20 AFTERMATHS

The consequential effects of this game are always staged in many forms by the fraudsters. Exposing dangers like murders, kidnaps, suicides, displacements, emotional disfiguring etc. But many prefer to stay backstage than bringing out their sad story to the public, for fear of exposure to disgrace, empty pity and remarkableness as to affect their societal status or company reputation. According to Wikipedia, the free encyclopedia, some of these individuals listed below, fell prey mercilessly.

Under kidnapping

Osamai Hitomi, a Japanese businessman.
Kenth Sadaaki Suzuki, a Swedish businessman.

Under murder
George Makronalli, a Greek man.
James Breaux, an American.

Furthermore, all is put in place by the con artists to see you collapse and fall never to rise again, even in body.

Their invitations are always garnered with all sorts of traps, because they are based in their territories and know their **"In- And- Out"**, to twist fact to their favor. They know how strict the law of their country is, when it comes to immigration. They lure you to come to their nation with mere accentuation on visa necessity and on your arrival difficulties are put in place with arrangements from those at the custom and visa control rooms to put particular attentions on you.

In that trick, makes it their preliminary reasons for the victim to spend a lot of money for his release or liberty. Then, easing his tension of wanting to reclaim the money if that was the motive coming to that nation. Or if insisting, go a-slaughtering with the victim; at certain height get you kidnapped or/and forced you, or your family out pay a ransom for your release, this is very common in Nigeria, South Africa and the world at large. It has made the US government under the department of secret service to assign agents to loiter around to protect and investigate matters of such caliber when their citizens are involved.

21 HOW MOST SCAMMERS END UP

Like any other game inspired from the devil, sure there is never a blissful ending with such beings practicing these arts. For tears of those who've been victims continue to pour not only from their faces but also from their hearts and souls. Unless, the victim is a notorious kind of criminal too or a harden sinner, so can we conclude that, you've been paid in your own coins. But when people hide behind the face of charity to extort on the pretext of higher money coming then know the end is near.

Experience has proven that, few 419ers really complete the life span projected to them naturally, and their family members are always target to the mark of their dishonesty, and at times innocently, they wonder into it. As people love and prefer to keep the surf of bad news.

Most of them end up in prison or die from untimely death provoked by repost of a duped person, police gunfire, altercation leading to murder, suicide or divine justice.

At times leading to a generational curse in a family, where plaguing in forms of diseases, strange deaths, victimization of monotonous injustice, perpetual poverty, family disunities, divorce or no marriages; in the evil men do, living after them.

But sadly enough, this con game is registering an alarming membership of new adepts every day, with Americans and Africans on the top list.

22 RECENT CYBER SCAMMING METHOD

1. Disbursement/Pay Out Of Money From Wills Scam: This is the disbursement proposal, whereby, the new heritor asks you to help him or her transfer the newly begotten fortune to your account, in return, will give you percentages, that are never fixed depending on the crook; followed often by advanced fee or many upfront fees for taxes etc.

2. Contract Fraud (C.O.D. of Goods or Services) Scam: The height of make-believe ballooned in the assurance that, all due money is given on the arrival of the goods. Firstly, this is with the initial attitude of an advanced fee which permits to precise over the necessary documents that would lead to the shipping of the goods. This is also applied to the express delivery scam, of paying the agency on the arrival of the goods at your home, by fake agents.

4. Transfer of Funds From Over Invoiced Contracts Scam: From the heading one can just feel the lame of the scheme. You are made to believe that, much money has been given as compared to the initial payment for a government contract, and immediate zeal is taken to evacuate the surplus abroad and to do so, one person must be at hand; called the prey or the victim to help make the magic happen; in multiple advance fees always the theory.

5. Sale of Crude Oil at Below Market Prices Scam: We all know how monetary this kind of domain can be like; with all international rules and regulations binding it trade. Correctly, in this era, where mineral resources are going out of reach, many companies find it hard to reach their usually expectations, and with a sudden proposal of such caliber from a country producing nation from a so-called **Crude-Oil- Producing-Body**, all reasons are there to get the optimum; at times to the level of displacing a person or persons to enhance the deal.

6. You Won Lottery Scam: To be frank dear readers, how on earth can you win something that you've never entered for it, if not a joke of a bad taste! For we all know that, they have never been any free launch on earth. For nothing has ever been due for nothing. Where, if you win, it means you played. People who fall for such scams are individuals with dollars stamps on their eyes, the masses or the daily consumers, who in everything around them having dollar's value. 419ers of this dominion concur collectively that, this philosophy of less gain is more rapid, than chasing a long list of zeros. At times not very sure, and with all sorts of risk and alarms around.

7. Transfer of Assets Scam: In the advent of some African countries internal conflicts, scammers use these tactics to lure people of possession of diamonds and gold, on the make believe that, they are chief rebels, families or potential individuals; or just stolen objects of high monetary value; and want to transfer their blood assets abroad in return for heavy benefits or percentages.

8. Purchase of Real Estate Scam: Gives space for the search of an agent and a near man to gain from the percentage being put forward. Where he is to search for an asset that is going to be bought, and own by the boss, of the proposer, usually a high personality in the government of that country. He is stimulated into the fact, it is a very top secret issue, because the person involved is a high personality and he, doing the deal with him is just an intermediary.

9. Hot And Heavy Accounts To Share Scam:
This scheme is often associated with wills
and inheritance scam. The victim is accosted
with the understanding, to extradite the
money very fast, due to heavy family
quarrels, menace to the throne, threat to his
life, because of his legality being next to kin,
and can gain much money from doing the
deal, if co-operate by giving vital information
directly linked to him. So much so that the
money will be flown to their account that`s
offshore for a better future.

10. Dead Foreigners Scam: this has two
itinerant, that's with the banker or bank
mentioned being indispensable; an expatriate
particularly from occidental, who've lost his
life in a plane crash, health, accident or any
misfortune that he has been victim of. To be
more updated, the dupes use current
information about misfortune incidents,
which must have passed, or been uncovered
on CNN (*Cable News Network*) etc. In the
make believe that, this one had no relative or

attachment of a type to benefit from his wealth, as a result, proposes a deal of fleeing the money abroad in the idea that, this one should act the relative, and money be shared amongst them.

11. 419 Scam/The Nigerian Connections/The Advance Fee Fraud: It is said to have begun around the early 1980's in Nigeria and has today reached billions of dollars story. It is over insistence with unsolicited mails like fax, letter and emails from Nigeria or West Africans and the world at large. And 419 is the section of Nigerian penal code that condemns this act. (*http://www.nigeria-law.org/Criminal%20Code%20Act-Part%20VI%20%20to%20the%20end.htm*).

You receive emails or SMS proposing business deals to you on various percentages. The power of this attitude has let them to big reassurance of what has turn to be *Nigeria Recovery Scam,* and according to INTERPOL submissions, the victims are re-scammed by the same group of dupes in the name of agents of the EFCC (*Economic and Financial Crime Commission*) or something else, coming to investigate the victim's case.

And like the formal skill, they find themselves being taxed an up-front fee on their request for the smooth tracking of the matter.

12. Pleas for Charitable Donations Scam: This goes forth as it name tells; masked with all sort of pitiable situations to drag monetary concern. This fraud has many faces, unlike the other scams, because, it gets itself updated by recent world affairs, of war, epidemic, abuse of human rights, natural disasters and dejections of all sorts. Predominantly, it's common in nations under natural and political turbulence of sorts.

13. Romance Scam: This is a 419 scheme of both genders, where the man seduces a woman or vice versa to a lusty point where he/she finds it hard to maintain his/her emotional balance (lovelorn), then the venom of extortion is concocted in; followed often by a good con of stuck check, having bank statement trouble, requesting immediate help. People always trapped in this form are always honest persons with a good, stable job or even a single parent, only searching for a soul mate.

This is how some of these contacts begin in dating sites

(*Hi dear, I am not happy because of my loneliness though very beautiful, lovely romantic girl, it will be a great pleasure to let you that When we truly realize that we are all alone is when we need others the most" so write to me through faithkamara1@yahoo.com so I can tell you more and more pictures. waiting for your email now on faithkamara1@yah oo.com I luv your picture.*)

This person is always the incarnation of the multi-visages doing the same game trick with a lot of persons round the globe or even with your friend or your neighbor. They suck most of their victims in chat rooms or free dating sites. Most often, when the trick is unmasked, the person threatens to expose with a blackmail of all sorts, using information gotten from victim during your discursions.

Another type most recent is the luring of a woman to fall into the dogma of his seduction, by being the first to send goods or presents worth chanting of gaiety. Here, he functions with accomplices who, descends to the woman's house with **DHL** suits (*badge*), or other form of fast express delivery suits, with a multitude of cartoons on C.O.D execution. When she pays for the delivery worth much money, ends up discovering that all in the cartoons were just a mass of assembled rubbish like stones, sand, etc. the scam here becomes officially the recovery fees begotten from the woman at delivery.

14. Work In A Hotel Abroad Scam: These mischief givers have now chosen to go for hotel recruitment, claiming hotels in Canada or Britain needs *main d`oeuvre* (people) from all round the globe particularly from poor nations to cross over and work for them, coupled with hot advantages like paying air ticket if need be, as a deduction will be made upon signing the contract. Here again, multi advance fees are demanded as the steps unfold ranging at times to one thousand dollars, using all legal documents to illustrate their fraud.

15. Domestic Animals Scam: Occidentals have an unimaginable love for pets, leaving them go as wide as making them their benefactor on their death bed. Strange but very true and real, as the money used only for animal care alone in developed nations like the US goes far beyond the annual budget of some poor nations like Togo etc. This grotesque love for domestic animals has inspired 419ers think twice and feel the need to invest on a smooth stratagem worth that lane.

These con artists use sites with free ads display with photos, precisely on pets that are very rare to find, or at very expensive prices, and make a cheap deal. Usually in this situation, the buyer is the one going to the seller and scammer. Here again advance fees is needed for taxes and legal documentations of movement from one nation to the other etc.

16. Intellect Exploitation or Brain Scam: People always love trenching holes to play over others I.Q. In the perpetual exploitation of their weakness to land for something they so much hold at heart. This particular form of scam is very much found in individuals launching literal contests of poetry, prose or drama etc. That incite people to register in the contest in return they receive a letter on which their piece of poem etc. has been chosen for publication. Marking you into their grand anthology, and urging you to buy a copy of what you, yourself have helped to build. Question! Where do the overall sales go to? See the number of contributors and non-contributors who've bought the copy worldwide. That's where the smoke of scamming starts oozing out, because in real sense of the matter, they are out to swell their pockets with others intellectuality and luring them again to buy it, and make the pioneers grotesquely rich.

The second part of this intellectual exploitation scam, rhyme with individuals, promising to give contracts of translations, proofreading, articles writing etc. When you're asked to first of all, go with a test work of some pages. Often, it's the work already you're doing, as you do it in form of a test.

When many people contact the provider for the job, what they do is that each person requesting is given three pages of text work and at the end of the day, nobody gains the work because it has been done freely via testing style.

This is because all these job seekers give their best to reach the optimum. And at the end, most of these malefactors literally disappear on claims that the project has been abandoned. Freelancers should always have a specific quantity of words they want to do as test work from the so-called literal employers, and learn to stick it, rather than following words like, *"if you do it well, we will have a long way to go and you will be pleased about it"*. Be pragmatic freelancers.

17. Weight Loss Scam: Due to excessive desire to cut in shape and look very sexy, over-weight physically looking human beings, have now felt themselves, put away by modern fashion desires. As the society, has not stopped talking about the dangers of elephant obesity ills.

And those who do not have means to meet *Dr. Rey* one on one, chooses the internet as their last options to command or order products that have little or no effect to their problem. Most often, fall on these lawbreakers that would paste photos begotten from individuals who've undergone the natural theory to reach, then would blind fool you to giving advance fees. In pay before reception policies, for it is a hot market.

18. Work At Home Scam: There is no wonder that the world is undergoing heavy economic cries, and those from developed world are greatly affected by this, as unemployment is rising up, day in, day out, seeing the kind of life style they were living before. It has become so hard that many have sided themselves with work at home opportunities to equilibrate things.

But, one question has predominantly remained, that of, do they really get their dues? This scam falls under one of the greatest 419 of our time. Because the desperate nature of people has pushed them so much into the buying of this option without really thinking if it is really a legitimate factor.

The system here is very smart and swift, the perpetrators makes a nation's tour of it companies , collect their addresses and their referrals, and pack fill in one block or CD, then starts selling via internet accosted by logos of famous medias networks like *CNN*, *NBC*, *TIMES* magazines to magnify that they are known. Most often without the notion of these companies or their permission, they even go as far promising money back guarantee.

It's purely *fake* and a way to attract, because none has ever really confirmed it, whether been given back money. This is fraud. They now operate with style of giving you an initial tariff and when decide to close the page, another payment option still shows up via what is call a *landing page*, with much lesser amount in a tiny rectangular page, and this goes up to third proposal even. That's initial pricing 99$, when want go away, breaks to 44$ and finally to 17$, dragging you by all means to fall for the swindle. Their sites are always decorated with flows of dollars, showing one or two faces claiming to be making 500$ or more in an hour,   an overzealous publicity that has no true foundation.

Their technology has gone higher, with sophisticated software that determines area and country of the person having access to their site, then automatically hoist your country's flag and showing a presume someone or a mother with a name perfectly from area claiming to be making fabulous gain an hour, assuring you that, you have all legal right to be part of the advantage. **Smart software for smart guys!**

19. Social Network Scam: Nowadays, some

outstanding social networks use their potentials to lure their members to filling surveys with believes that they have hot videos of celebrity in nude or sex tape newly release. Brief, this means that, they ask you to answer questions for the survey and which at the end, you're served the desire.

This is brainy done, the team hook up a scheme of making a comment on your friend`s behave and you seeing it, gets immediately enticed to wanting to discover what is in that tape. By the time you're done with the survey either you're informed that your country is not liable, or you've not got the necessary software to view the video or something to discourage you in the whole shell. And we all know, such surveys don't go with the company involve not paying heavily. One of these cases was seen with *Nikki Minaj* presume sex tape scandal that turn the whole fans roaming on *Facebook*. And all was in a hurry to see, but found themselves doing smooth surveying.

20. Ponzi Scam: In this pattern, you are promised higher earnings as compare to the usual ways of functioning. That's the dividends are more in percentage as compare the vestment made, usually by the acts of paying money to the initial investors with sums begotten from the latest partners, in a con gesture of proximity and measuring on the numbers of investors.

And when the members decide to turn their backs by quitting the firm with nothing to pay the recently entered, the whole thing then goes to water, simple reason practical investment does really exist, and rather betting on the amount of people willing to join. Founded in the early 1900's by Charles Ponzi, a Bostonian from Massachusetts; a system still making heavy victims today.

23 GENERAL TIPS FOR FIGHTING CYBER SCAM

Please for God sake, always stop and asked yourself these vital questions. Why on earth would a real stranger choose you to share in a windfall of millions? Why a perfect stranger for you?

Why on earth, would you give out your top placed information, like bank account numbers, your company letterhead, phone number, address and more just on a make believe by someone totally out of your reach? Why?

Why on earth would you send him money, as an advance fee or a multiple up-front fees just on a make believe? Why?

Why on earth would you give too much room to a real stranger and to end up witnessing threats, kidnap, debts, stress, confusion, extortions, murder or assignations? Why!

By the time you read these tips, much about your sentiments to venture this type of business will surely change.

1)   Remember! Nothing is ever it in the internet, till it is really it. *Rule number one*. Take it like an illusion at first sight. Forget the notoriety.

2)   Never, never, never be in a haste while doing any online business particularly with a body typically anew to you. Never! Always put aside their reputation study how and where you must go in; for their fraud can begin with you.

3)   Try as hard as possible to know with

whom you're treating with. It will be unwise and unfair for you to throw trust, just like that, pending on a make believe. Carry on a thorough investigation in *Google, Ask, Bing, AltaVista* search engine, and compare the credentials step by step (*emails, fragments of messages etc.*) Pose questions and be very attentive to the responding, as scammer might try to drag your attention off, in introducing stages of different conversation.

4)   Be smart and a follow-up type of person. As most of their emails are stereo-tape type and anything out of line brings trouble. Consult sites that are related to 419ers exposed like
 www.419scammersexposed.com,
www.aa419.org and **www.Hoaxbuster.com** etc. That has exposed a lot of scammers particularly from Africa with pictures begotten from *Facebook* etc.

5)   The weight of the business might be so high and as a result, you might be tempted to

travel to the country of business location. First thing to do is to make sure that your entourage is consulted, that's your lawyer, banker and the security business organization involved. Be an adept of reason, rather than desire.

6)   Make sure your travelling documents are all in norms, especially your medications certificates, visa stamp etc. This is because; every possible error can be used as a weapon against you. For it is part of their tactics, to be always in connivers with their milieu.

7) Don't allow your desire to surpass your reasoning just because the figures assure you windfall gains. Make sure the business is well comprehended by you or consult an attorney, expert in the field, forget about this issue of confidentiality, it is their first ruse to guarantee your brain washing and shut up. Be a man and take risk, by talking to others who can orientate you.

8)   As mentioned up, they (*419ers*) use this

tactic of utmost confidentiality or *non-disclosure* to captivate your common sense or sense of alert. Shaping things to be very hard for you to go down true verifications as it is merited.

In some cases, they even menace with law suit, if you breach the agreement, by wanting to air out your losses to the body concern. Laugh on that and get on with your intending, for a true thief will never come out to light.

9)   Don't get influenced by these issues, their race, nationality, education, age or gender. Forget about common errors you might encounter in the communication letters, or emails, which usually finds it place only in the mid corners of the messages, proving their intellectuality only on a proportion, all these are swindles or hide-behind ways by these con-artists to make you feel superior and later deal with you in the proper remedy.

These guys are professionals in their acts but you must be alert to trace their demi-senses. Never pay a penny till it is cash on delivery, which of course will never be so, as all lies under fake and theft.

10) Give more hardness to your passwords. It should have at least a minimum of eight characters, combined with upper and lower case characters, not putting aside the use too of a number or more.

And don't use the same password on all your dating sites or popular sites. So too, your email password should be different from your *Facebook* own, likewise the others, to avoid unnecessary hacking to your privacy by email sellers and internet fraudsters.

11) Avoid trading of all sorts with individuals giving no direct information on their **post office** or **street address**, straight **phone** lines; for a serious person or company

begins with those vital acquisitions. It is but obvious that, this attitude lingers to a well label conning, when never on the spot for an answering of his phone calls, but prefers answering machine to get to you later. Honestly, does this sound normal, if really you are a true client for his deal? As these are *mise-en-scene* (*setups*) of inns and taverns brought to city area, still wearing it original scent and demands; just little attention from your common sense to track them out, is required.

12) Protect your computer from all sorts of evil. Make your email a thing for you and your VIPS. That's friends and relations. Use software that fights virus and spams. Install a firewall and never allow an automatic entry by leaving your computer to have an **auto-recall** of your passwords. This is very dangerous, as it might open the get way for fraudsters. And don't remain log-in perpetually in a website. You must learn to have an autonomous control of all your

cyberic endeavors.

13) Still in this line of alert, quit phone calls with beginnings 003, 004, 005, 006, 008, 00225, 00229. These guys are very agile and won't go with what will in any way put them at risk and if they are using a particular number with you and are discovered by the victim as being con artist, immediately throw away the SIM CARD using.

That's why a true 419er must always go with four to five telephone numbers at his disposal. For the intermediary voice is often him, in another voice to make you believe or go in association with an occidental Caucasian to erase you off suspicion, if it is a *West African* scammer or the other.

Indeed earning for the white dude a percentage from the harvest. This is very common with affaires of heavy means.

14)   Don't allow the person to dominate your spirit by being totally real in all his approaches. Don't allow him to put pressure on you unnecessarily. His cleanliness must be strangeness to you till proven merited. Develop that habits of always finding errors or dig one by all means crucial, because as you do, will you surely witness or discover issues of questionable height.

15)   Have the habit of always wanting to see his main website, his affiliations with popular social networks like Facebook, Skype, LinkedIn, Twitter plus his partners. If in case, he is unable to produce at least two of these sites, Skype and Facebook.

Doubt him and watch your steps, as businesses round the globe all have it and is profiting via paying or free mode advantages of these networks. As these sites are channels that permit him (*trader*) to be in permanent contact with his clients round the globe in all direct video discursion, commentaries.

16) Schemers like those of *work at home* theory have this funny trick of always pasting on their sites *Money Back Guarantee.* America having one of the biggest economic trouble of the century, has seen a heavy loss of jobs of it time resulting too to many tilting themselves in this option and ending with little or no result of satisfaction nor money refunded, marking one of the greatest frauds of our time.

Please, abstain from falling for such cheap ruse of theirs, do your jobs search in a formal and acceptable way. Instead, they have a very malicious way of doggedness for you to buy the offer through instantaneous money reduction windows (**Landing Page**) as you show indefatigability to go away.

They function in many dimensions, they collect anonymously names and contacts of business sites, pill them up in one disk, write instructive lines on how to do it, create powerful banners, formulate a powerful scenario of the author`s success or another person's story with photos, sitting in front rented/borrowed expensive cars.

Next, victims are numbered upon release in the internet. Some have even grown sophisticated, having immediate chat system upon notice of your presence in their site and if venture to reply, witness a massive persuasiveness to buy their option, as price options continue to grow smaller as you attempt to quit the website.

This is a pure American form of 419, using originality to make believe that non Americans too, can also be part of the cake, as a result, many from poor nations also fall victim. Believing that, dollars will change their lives as compare to the low currency of their country.

17) Use websites with apt software to track down their IP (*http://www.wikihow.com/Trace-*

an-IP-Address,http://forums.whatismyipaddress.com/viewforum.php?f=7). Through the email you're being given or treating with him. Do it as many times as you can, and if any fluctuation or over fluctuation, please hold your steps.

As you must never let him know that you're doing all these behind his back or as powerful as he is in his ability to stray you apart, will fabricate a burning strategy to make you grow cold and docile for him to suckle you to your doom as was his initial plan. Even though the site won't give you all about his address when tracking, at least his location will be indicated to you, that's, the town, city, time and date, for you to confirm his words. It's very simple.

18) Do have the decency of not often relying on business transactions made through money exchange program. For instance, popular money exchange companies like **Western Union, Money Gram** have this

popular policy of round the globe money withdrawal, permitting you to withdraw money sent to you from any part of the world.

This, has made cyber scam very organized, as you need not be exactly where you made believe, to lure a person's fortune. In another word, your neighbor can be the one killing you. Watch out, ample care should be given to this form of dealing. It is their transaction policy and none can contradict it.

19) The person in the name of an **Interlocutor**. This third party, as seen in the explanations above, is that individual who comes in when the deal is gone the next level, where the victim receives courier from the rogue.

All of these can be in the form of a banker, an agent of clearing house, factually, nailing some cautionary spirit and alert which ought to be taken seriously; of always going with a lot of precautions and slowness, because, these guys are often the accomplices of the scammer sharing the same confrere motives.

20) Let's be in the real definition of the parley, why should a citizen of a country, and being in that country, finds it hard to articulate in the proper dialect of the place. Why should his accent don't concord with his place of stay?

It brings a lot of pathos to the soul to see that very common ways are used to abuse the intellect of well-read human beings. You must be on the cruise of your senses, as you do international business with individual who claims to be of particular nationality.

You must learn to pose initial questions and make him answer you directly of his identity and anything of doubt, stop the deal immediately or give yourself more time to think over. True, everybody cannot be smart at once, but get yourself formed by learning about the realities of the milieu and this is one good reason, this book has been written.

21) Beware of some professions! There are some individuals that come in the form of religious men (*priest, pastors etc.*), as attorneys, as diplomat, as notables, occupations that gives little or no quest to wanting to put trust to question. A 419er will pass through any door to get anything he wants if that won't hurt him.

They try by all means available to be clean on time. These goes alongside individuals claiming to be the survivors of natural disaster like the case of **Haiti**. This is where fraudsters saw it a very obvious means to eat money from their stools at home. You can only give monetary help only through well-known organization doing it in your country or in your region. Or if the amount you to want give is too large, then divide it to many of such organizations doing the sending to that same nation.

22) Dramatic stories of doubtful origin must not have effect on you. Mere cyber correspondence must not extend strings or lead to over sudden issues requesting immediate financial help. Like health case, problem with the law, travel issues of Visa request, investment etc. Put in your mind that, that age has passed for such swindles and you're immune to it.

In front of such demands from an unknown person, simply refer him/them to Google, Bing search, because they are the cradle of information and reference of such caliber. You must learn to be very pragmatic in what you do and how you help.

Be very concrete of where and how you got the information with physical referrals. Though it does not guarantee all assurance but at least, you have a clue if you want size them up, and know how they look like.

23) Learn to be on the one eye sleep tact. Be a person of due diligence, and master the acts of good investment. Be an unfailing referrer; in as much as you might be confronted with individuals claiming to be government representatives. In suggesting capital flight (*from Princely wealth, dead-bed-declared fortunes, war zone discovered gold, overpaid government contracts, diamonds*); in return, for fabulous sums of gain, worth millions of dollars. For these are always wolves dressed in sheep clothing.

The instance, they've got your bank account number, your address, telephone number, you are in big trouble in your own country and in your own space. In other words, experience has proven that we're all gluttons, overeaters, foodie, gorger in one way or the other when money is concern, in every human being a hot percentage.

Thereby invoking, we should learn to control that ego when comes to cyber business with impostors. As we all know from the Wise's parleys, there is no free lunch and has never been.

24) Please, from the courtesy of the 419 Coalition, in response to the attitude to adopt when venturing business with Nigerian and West Africans a large. Though we must have echoed it in many forms, but yet take it again in an official manner.

They emphasis, *never pay any up- front fee no matter the reasons, never extend credit for any reasons no matter the pressure put forward, never forward any amount of money till your banker confirms that the check has been cleared, never expect any form of assistance from the Nigerian government or the other, never rely on your government to bail you out if gotten into hot trouble of the trick.* This is very serious and a pure warning from above.

25)   Another bloody scheme by these bad guys passes through spam emails. You stylishly receive emails as if were from official online banks (*PayPal, eBay, eMoney*) in the name of a merchant. Requesting you confirm your personal information.

This is a very big trap, if you had no dealings of such, why give away your private information just because you've been made to believe in money that you know nothing about.

Please, learn to make your information your soul's secrets. Secondly, you might receive an email from any pay online site, complaining of overdue money in your online account or unexpected taxes that you must pay through money exchange like **Western Union, MoneyGram** etc. Please be on the watch point, things don't operate that way, rather than do that, go to the main site where all started and get you confirmed the email.

26) Widen your imagination and creativity. Try from all faculties to read from the books and internet, of the risk involved in the form of deal you about to get into. The internet has freely, all the *pros* and *cons* of what we intend to do or at least a clue.

It is an **encyclopedia** for proper understanding of every existing case. So, instead of venturing a grandiose risk by freely giving out your vital facts relating to your private life and your economies or wealth, just go ahead and create a different identity and account.

Then, wait till your banker confirms to you that the check or money wired is **REAL** for usage. If not so, never take any step from agitations of yours, because you might regret bitterly.

Better lose two thousand dollars in creating a barrier of security for yourself and family than throw hundreds of thousands of dollars on a make believe and selling your souls to everlasting grief, debts, law breakings, quarrels or even suicide or murder instinct.

27) Okay, because letting them have a hold of you in your vital codes, bank account number, just merely grant an open corridor for schemes like suggesting you depositing foreign check then lure you contribute for some recounted vital expenses, for example, the con-artist sends you a check of 50.000dls then sooner ask you to forward him 10.000dls on behave of some expenses worth handling.

With certitude in you, in a couple of days' time, the check sent to you by him will be confirmed into your account, when only to ascertain that, it will take you an eternity to reach, as your bank starts requesting answers for bank statement.

28) Most of these guys move around often, with stolen identities, as they specialize in

creating temporal commercial accounts round the nation or even out, permitting them cash bogus checks deposited easily by them, then disappear without being traced.

But those with little agility or financial acceleration go fast, quick and end with a balance account upon done with the victim. What do we mean here, single and static scammers prefer to put an end, when immediately sting a victim through the use of a balance account as compare to the one with ability to exercise nomadic attitude, with big means.

29) Immediately you realize that you've been victim of fraud, having given all your vital information, call fast your banker and tell him to have a close look at your account henceforth. Don't waste time, and if you're lucky by this time, all can still be intact, but in some cases, before the eye opens up, the story is the contrary.

Again, create a new account when dealing with online business, and if he transfer the money anyway, which of course can never be possible, because there is none, sit on it and fold your arms to see him claim it back.

30) Certain downloading might be very dangerous, be very alert on what you CLICK open and distribute. Safe openings, goes forth with these brands **bmp, jpg, gif, png, tiff, jpeg, tga** and then quit ones like **scr or exe.**

31) Do not use public **WI-FI** in carrying out vital dealings, like bank issues, buying issues, contract discursion etc. Don't give your personal contacts through emails you suspect not real, as most big companies dealing online will hardly bombard you with emails requesting this or that. If in that kind of dilemma, just call the company involved and verify directly. Than risk a whole life's economy.

24 COUNTER-ATTACK PRAYERS OF OUR LORD JESUS CHRIST

The only way we can fight evil, is by calling on the Child of God Jesus Christ, to come to our rescue. He is the light and the only way. He, who, passes through him gains eternal life and protection. These prayers can be said before entering into a deal, during a deal or after even been a victim. God can still operate for you in many ways to make your heart turn cold. But, it is very much better while entering a deal, particularly if you doubt yourself. Asking guidance and protection against evil influence, for its only by the grace of God which you can pass through the hands of these guys or else by will or force their will sweep you.

Many things can be as a result to our victimization, reasons I have personality gathered prayers related to all our actual troubles, that can lead to us being victim to Satan`s ruse. These prayers were personally given by our lord himself. Please, say them (prayers) with a lot of devotion and adoration for the one who died for us to be saved, if possible on your knees, because they`re too powerful and falls under the greatest devotion of our generation. All he needs is sincerity, true love and complete contrition of our sins, and you might see miracles operating.

THE MYSTICAL PRAYERS OF OUR LORD JESUS CHRIST (On your knees if possible)

I.   OPENING

God come to my aide

Lord, to our help

Glory be to the father, to the son and to the Holy

Spirit

To God who is, who was, and who cometh

Forever and ever, Amen

II. All you great numerous enemies; the enemy of the holy death of my Master Jesus Christ on the Cross of Calvary; the prince of darkness and iniquity, the father of all liars; I stand on the death of my Master Jesus Christ and offer His pains, wounds, and the Precious Blood of His left hand to the Eternal Father for your downfall, your destruction and your scourging. Amen. Precious Blood of my Master Jesus Christ - reign in me and in the lives of all men. Amen.

III. Adoration! Adoration!! Adoration!!! To Thee, O powerful weapon. Adoration! Adoration!! Adoration!!! To Thy Precious Blood.
Merciful Agonizing Jesus Christ, pour Your Precious Blood on our souls. Satisfy my thirst and defeat our enemies. Amen.

Powerful Blood of salvation, fight the enemy. (3 times) L: Precious Blood of Jesus Christ

R: Save us and the whole world. (12 times) Glory Be*...
(Bow Your Head)

May the Precious Blood that pours out from the Sacred Head of Our Lord Jesus Christ, the Temple of Divine Wisdom, Tabernacle of Divine Knowledge and Sunshine of heaven and earth, cover us now and forever. Amen.

25 HOW TO COMPLAINT

As said in the introduction of this book, 419 is like software which undergoes fast updating day in, day out. Since victims are always there to be tap freely earth wise, confirming that it is just enough for one brotherhood to develop a new style, all the rest will follow overnight and before it reaches the Interpol awareness or the FBI or local police of the milieu at times, or if they are found in less develop country, the temptation can be very high and most often than not, the cops succumbs to the money bribe rather than handing the culprits when apprehended.

Even in the visage of reality and justice,

some captured individuals immediately make use of their high place contacts, with just a phone call, the twist is done. As we all know most governments or police to be the most corrupt body on earth. Yet, it's very much advisable to forward your complain. As light can always shine on your case.

a) Gather all references made to you in terms of emails sent (*with the message's full header information*), since day one of your communication, if possible with date references too. As this will help track it originality.

b) Collect all references relating to all money transfer made (receipts etc.) that confirms your sending.

c) The name or a list of names of people contacted (nicknames used, fax, phone numbers, copies of couriers inter changed, if possible recorded phone calls.

419 THE CYBERSCAM GAME

d) Adding all vital forms of information that can be helpful like description of his voice or noted attitude when talking etc.   . (http://www.straightshooter.net/help_for_fra ud_victims.htm).

26 WHERE TO FILE A COMPLAINT

Filing a complaint always goes alongside with a lot of pains and regret. Beneath it, the truth still holds it grounds, as the probability of apprehending the culprits is always very dim. As minor cases are not always taken seriously by the bodies involved till the sums start talking about hundreds of thousands of dollars. Worst still, if the culprits are based abroad and in a far continent like Africa, it becomes a closed topic as you turn your back. As the assurance of recuperating the money becomes very impossible, even in the capture of the bandits.

1) To Nigerian Economic and Financial Crime Commission (EFCC). at http://www.efccnigeria.org/

2) To Nigerian Embassy or high commission in your country of reside.

3) To National Law Enforcement Agency and National foreign Office in your country.

4) To Spam-cop that has the ability to track the fraudsters emails accounts despite the ISP they are using and landing to their initial point of debut.

5) To Yahoo provider. abuse@yahoo.com; alongside its header, requesting it closure.

6) To Google or Gmail provider. abuse@gmail.com; alongside its header, requesting it closure.

7) To Hotmail provider. abuse@hotmail.com. Alongside its header, requesting it closure.

8) To the US Secret Service.

9) To local FBI office.

10) To the U.S. Postal Inspection Service.

11) Federal Trade Commission's Complaint Assistance. (spam@uce.gov).

12) To INTERPOL (International Police).

13)   BEFTI (Brigade d'Enquêtes sur les Fraudes aux Technologies de l'Information).

163 avenue d'Italie, 75 013 Paris.

14) To eBay spoof@ebay.com (emails related to eBay).

15)   To PayPal spoof@paypal.com (emails related to PayPal).

16)   To Citi emailspoof@citigroup.com

(emails related to Citi).

.

17) The Internet Crime Complaint Center (IC3).

18) Central Bank of Nigeria. Anti-corruption Unit at anticorruptionunit@cenbank.org and should do so especially if CBN is mentioned in the 419 materials.

19) For Australians. Australian West African Organized Crime Section at (er-waoc@afp.gov.au).

20) For Belgians. Belgian Federal Police at contact@fccu.be.

21) For Canadian nationals or citizens. Phonebusters info@phonebusters.com or the Royal Canadian Mounted Police Website (RCMP/GRC)For Netherlands. To the Fraud Department of the National Criminal Intelligence Service of the Netherlands ("subject should be APOLLO – LOSS

"WACN@klpd.politie.nl') Project Apollo (LOSS or NO LOSS). Korps Landelijke Politiediensten, Postbus 3016, 2700 KX Zoetermeer, The Netherlands, Telephone no. : 0031- 79- 3458900, Fax.no. : 0031- 79- 3459100.

22) For South Africans. to the Commercial Branch, South African Police Service, Head Office for attention Superintendent SC Schambriel at facsimile number +27 12 339 1202, telephone number + 27 12 339 1203 or e-mail hq.commercial@saps.org.za. Please mention whether or not you have incurred any financial loss.

23) For the British. The London Metropolitan Police website section concerning fraud:

.

http://www.met.police.uk/fraudalert/419.htm

.

27 TOP SITES EXPOSING SCAMMERS WORLDWIDE

Scam emails, multi-telephone numbers etc.

a)   **www.419scammersexposed.com**

b)   **www.aa419.org**

c)   **www.Hoaxbuster.com**

28 TOP STATISTIC SITES

Usually cyber-crimes are often a harden type of statistic to gather due to it vastness and earth wise strings. But most often, it is from the various complaints gathered yearly that, an outstanding estimation can be made that goes at times with the different bodies involved. Amongst perpetrators 85percent are men and most reside in the US and amongst complainants 65percent are men.

Particularly individuals from working class based in potential economic countries. £1bn a year, according to Western Union and the Office of Fair Trading stands as the exact estimate of money burgle from victims via it system. Making it a vital reasons, for her to join in the fight for this epidemic by asking all clients to fill a form assuring that they ain't a trapped of any form of swindle, boosting the vigilance of it staffs over the issue. But all these for how long, because they now accomplices in some countires.

a. Estimated least loss per person in
- America, Europe, and some Asia countries (India, Thailand, Singapore etc.)=1700dls.

- Africa and very poor nations a large= 300dls.

b. Top 419 nations in the world with America top leading.
United States , United Kingdom, Nigeria, Canada, China, South Africa, Ghana, Spain, Italy, Romania, Philippines, Israel, Cameroon, Malaysia, Brazil, Spain, France, Turkey, Poland, India, Pakistan, Russia, South Korea, Taiwan, Japan, Mexico,

Argentina, Australia, Germany.

29 SAMPLES OF RECENT 419 LETTERS

i)
Hi Friend,

How are you? Guess you are fine and living good, nice having your address with the aid of my new search device, my name is Claret Anitson a citizen of United States of America, i was born in
1982.

I am here just looking for better friendship and pen pals both women and men to share interest and lot more with, i love discussing all issues and learning other people's cultures and languages, hope to get more good and lasting friends outside my state, friends are like cloths, and life is naked without one.

About me in a brief, my names are miss Claret Anitson a native of United States of America, and i am working with a recruitment and resettlement agency here in (UK), i think it is enough for now till i hear from you, now tell me about yourself and your country.

Plz excuse me if i erred by contacting you in this mail, you can forward my message to any of your preferred mailbox and reply via it for easier correspondence,

Will be expecting to hear from you soonest, till then bye. Your new friend,
Miss Claret Anitson

Hello ,

Glad knowing you. I am not concerned about your nationality, race, age and religion. Friendship has not language "friendship is a symbol of eternity that wipes away all sense of time, How strong are you in the things of God.
removing all memory of a beginning and all fear of an end." Age does not protect you from love.I wishes you merry Xmas and New Year in Advance.
but love to some extent protects you from age I am Nancy Jack 26 yrs old from California in the United States of America
Well I am a happy woman who enjoys life in all its forms. I have a very fulfilling job where I work with amazing people each day. I have a family
I adore and who reminds me each time I see them how great life can be. I surround myself with a great group of positive thinking friends who would do anything for me, and I would do anything for them in return. I
enjoy being in a crowd at times, but I enjoy spending time with only a few people as well. I love to travel and see new places, so I try to travel as much as I can especially on official duties. I have learned to take life as it happens as I remember everything happens for a reason.
My hobbies are reading, watching movies, swimming, listening to music and traveling.
Try and reach me through my email address so that i can send my photographs to you
Yours
Nancy

ii)   Bonjour cher

Mon nom est Mlle Prisca j'ai vu votre profil aujourd'hui à www.tagged.com et s'intéresse, veuillez Madame, Monsieur, je serai très heureuse si vous pouvez me contacter directement avec ce mon email (missprisca1988@yahoo.com) ce que je vais vous dire plus sur une image pour que vous sachiez qui je suis et moi (n'oubliez pas que la distance ou la couleur n'a pas d'importance mais amour compte beaucoup dans la vie). J'espère pouvoir lire bientôt, à partir d'u
Merci   de   Mlle   Prisca.
missprisca1988@yahoo.com

....

Hello dear
My name is Miss Prisca ,i saw your profile today at www.tagged.com and became interested , Please dear , i will be very happy if you can contact me direct   with   this   my   email (missprisca1988@yahoo.com)
so that i will tell you more about myself and a picture for you to know whom i am (remember that distance or color does not matter but love matters a lot in life) .

I hope to read from u soon ,
Thanks from
Miss Prisca .

missprisca1988@yahoo.com

Dearest Lovely One.

I'm happy to inform you about my success in getting those funds transferring under the cooperation of a new partner from London UK. Presently I'm in UK with my Lovely Husband for investment projects with my own share of the total sum.meanwhile,i didn't forget your past efforts and attempts to assist me in transferring those funds despite that it failed us somehow.

Now contact Rev Emmanuel James, (**rev_fatheremmanuel.lordservice@yahoo.com**) ask him to send you the total cheque Draft of $350.000 (three hundred and fifty thousand dollars) i purposely drop this cheque in your favor for your compensation for all the past efforts and attempts to assist me in this matter.i appreciated your efforts at that time very much, so feel free and get in touched with the Rev father Emmanuel James and on how to send the bank draft cheque to you.You may not hear from me again because my Husband are ready for us to travel out of London UK for vacation so please try and make sure that you get this bank draft cheque out from Rev father you can only go little process to have the cheque i made it for security purpose in your name. I'm very busy here because of the investment projects which me and the new partner/Husband are having at hand, finally,remember that i had forwarded instruction to the Rev Father Emmanuel James on your behalf to receive that money, so feel free to get in touch with the Rev Father without any delay.

Best
regards,
Mrs
Blessing,
I am Married now

Hello,

I saw your profile.

I am writing to you because I have aproblem.

I do not know how to explain it to you... I hope I can

trust you. I am a little short of funds to finish my

studies.

I am in need of just few Euros. I will be very
thankfull if you can mail me 5 Euros.

It is less that a price of colour magazine.

It would be a great help for me (almost as matter
of life and death).

In exchange I will send you over 200 unpublished
pictures of myself.

Here are some samples:

http://faphost.in/1

cafab

http://faphost.in/0

k4am1

http://faphost.in/cfcgvd

http://faphost.in/51iqhv

I belive that I did not offended you with this

request. If anyway you feel uneasy with

that. I am very sorry.

But if you decide to help me, do write and I will
send you all details.

I will guarantee honesty. With best wishes

Hello,

Glad knowing You. I am not concerned about your nationality, race, age and religion. Friendship has not language "friendship is a symbol of eternity that wipes away all sense of time,
removing all memory of a beginning and all fear of an end." Age does not protect you from love
but love to some extent protects you from age. I am Joan Harry 30 yrs
old from Kentucky in the United States of America
Well I am a happy lady who enjoys life in all its forms. I have a very fulfilling job where I work with amazing people each day. I have a family I adore and who reminds me each time I see them how great life can be. I surround myself with a great group of positive thinking friends who would do anything for me, and I would do anything for them in return. I enjoy being in a crowd at times, but I enjoy spending time with only a few people as well. I love to travel and see new places, so I try to travel as much as I can especially on official duties. I have learned to take life as it happens as I remember everything happens for a reason.
My hobbies are reading, watching movies, swimming, listening to music and traveling.
"The essential sadness is to go through life without loving. But it would be almost equally sad to leave this world without ever telling those you loved that you love them.
"Sometimes the one thing you are looking for; is the one thing you can't see."
The type of man who attracts me is honest, direct, and

reliable - who can be my "pal". I like a man who's playful one minute, and philosophical the next. Above all, companionship, honesty, and idealism appeal to me - and a sense of humor! My ideal partner is a very passionate person who knows how to fully enjoy life. has a highly active imagination when it comes to trying new things. More than most people, he knows how to value the pleasures of romance and is not afraid to pursue those feelings when the timing is right. He also has a strong intellect, with a penetrating thought process and a continual curiosity about the world around him. I like treating my partner well and also like to be treated as one. My instincts tells me you have all this qualities in you,you are welcome to my world and I will send you my photographs in my next mail.I am hoping to
hear from you. Love is a gift;Yet love is a debt. Take the gift of my love and pay your debt when love calls.

Thanks
Joan.

From: Western Union®
<wu.transferdesk@w.cn> Sent: Wed, April 6,
2011 9:37:32 AM
Subject: CONDUCT CODE (303)

WESTERN UNION HEAD OFFICE
DEPARTMENT REPUBLIC OF BENIN.
FOREGN CONTRACTOR PAYMENT OFFICE
TELEPHONE +229-96846005

WEB SITE.www.westernunion.com

GOOD DAY MY DEAR,
MAY ALMIGHTY FATHER BLESS YOU FOR ALL YOUR
EFFORT AND PRAYER CONCERN ME, I JUST
RETURNED FROM HOSPITAL YESTERDAY MORNING.
THOUGH I WAS NOT TOO WELL BUT I HAVE TO
REQUEST FOR DISCHARGE AS I KNOW THAT GOD
ALMIGHTYT FATHER WILL HEAL THE REST,

I AM PLEADING TO YOU IN THE NAME OF GOD
BECAUSE IT HAS BEEN A WHILE NOW THAT WE DID
NOT COMMUNICATE, I HOPE THAT THINGS IS
MOVING NORMAL? HOWEVER I DECIDE TO WRITE
YOU AND VERIFY IF YOU HAVE RAISE THE $85.00
WHICH
I TOLD YOU TO PAY BEFORE LEFT TO HOSPITAL SO
THAT WE
CAN COMPLETE THE ASSIGNMENT WE HAVE AT
HAND.NOW TELL ME, HAVE YOU RAISED THE
$85.00 IF YES PLEASE SEND IT IMMEDIATELY SO

THAT MY EFFORT WILL BEEN COMPLETED.

I TRIED TO CALL YOU DURING MY STAY IN THE HOSPITAL BUT I CAN SEE THAT YOU PHONE IS HAVING PROBLEM. PLEASE MAKE SURE YOU WILL SEND THE MONEY FOR THE TRANSFER CHARGE BECAUSE YOUR PAYMENT IS ALREADY AVAILABLE TO PICK UP NOW TO YOU AND IT WILL START BY TOMORROW MORNING ONCE YOU SEND THE TRANSFER CHARGE TODAY.

I BELIEVE YOU KNOWS THAT THE NEEDED AMOUNT IS $185.00
BUT I ADVISE YOU TO SEND ONLY $85.00 THEN RETURN BALANCE OF $100.00 AFTER YOU RECEIVE FIRST PAYMENT OF
$1500.00 DOLLARS BY TOMORROW BUT PLEASE DON'T DELAY BY SENDING THIS $85.00 TODAY BECAUSE WE ALREADY POST YOUR FIRST PAYMENT TODAY AND AS SOON AS WE RECEIVE THE $85.00 FOR TRANSFER FEE WE WILL RELEASE THE FULL INFORMATIONS FOR YOU TO PICK UP $1500.00 BY TOMORROW
MORNING BEFORE 11 AM OUR TIME FROM ANY WESTERN UNION IN YOUR COUNTRY WITHOUT ANY DELAY AND WE WILL ALSO GIVE ANOTHER PAYMENT BY NEXT TOMORROW.

I SWEAR TO GOD ALMIGHT THAT $85.00 IS FOR TRANSFER CHARGE AND ONLY MONEY THAT YOU

HAVE TO SEND TILL YOU RECEIVE ALL YOUR PAYMENTS BEFORE YOU CAN PAY THE REMAIN BALANCE OF $100.00 BUT DON'T DELAY BY SEND THE

$85.00 TODAY BECAUSE THE PAYMENT WILL START AS FROM

TOMORROW MORNING BEFORE 11 AM OUR TIME ? SEND IT THROUGH WESTERN UNION WITH THIS INFORMATION BELOW:

1. RECEIVER NAME=======YOUNG SOLOMON
2.   CITY/COUNTRY=======COTONOU_BENIN REPUBLIC.
3. QUESTION===========IN GOD
4. ANSWER============WE TURST
5. AMOUNT============US$85.00

AS SOON AS YOU MAKE THE PAYMENTR PLEASE SEND AN EMAIL WITH THE WESTERN UNION PAYMENT INFORMATIONS SO THAT WE CAN PICK UP THE MONEY IMMEDIATELY AND GIVE YOU THE INFORMATIONS TO PICK UP YOUR $1500.00 IMMEDIATELY.

BE REST ASSURED THAT $85.00 IS FOR TRANSFER FEE AND IS

ONLY MONEY THAT YOU HAVE TO PAY AS FOR NOW TILL YOU RECEIVE ALL THE PAYMENTS THEN YOU CAN RETURN THE REMAIN BALANCE OF $100.000 OKAY SO GO AHEAD NOW TO MAKE THE PAYMENT IMMEDIATELY THROUGH WESTERN UNION, AFTER SENDING THE $85.00 PLEASE GIVE US 2HOURS

AHEAD TO YOUR FIRST PAYMENT THROUGH WESTERN UNION OKAY.
THEN AFTER TRACING IT JUST GO AHEAD AND SEND THE $85.00
IMMEDIATELY SO THAT WE CAN GIVE YOU THE REMAINGS INFORMATIONS TO PICK UP YOUR $1500.00 WITHIN 2HOURS YOU SEND THE MONEY.

I AM LOOKING FORWARD TO HEAR FROM YOU ONCE YOU RECEIVE THIS MAIL WITH THE PAYMENT INFORMATIONS OKAY?

Further more, you need to send total sum of $65,00,to use it for Transfer Charge your fund release MTCN,because,the Control numbers information, which you would be using to picking all your fund has been registered reference, If you calculate what we have putting in will know that you have gone too far to quit, After the payment sum of $65,00 the last number would release to you once you have made the payment.

MAY THE ALMIGHT FATHER BLESS

YOU. MR.JOHN AFAM.
WESTERN UNION HEAD OFFICE DEPARTMENT
REPUBLIC OF BENIN.
FOREGN CONTRACTOR PAYMENT
OFFICE THIS IS OUR CONDUCT
CODE (303) No_10_Achimota Road
Accra Ghana Republic of Ghana West
Africa.

RABIU MOHAMMED & CO
SOLICITORS & ATTORNEYS
60A ABUBAKAR WAY
VICTORIA ISLAND,
LAGOS - NIGERIA.
FROM THE DESK OF: **TEL/FAX: 234-**
90402708
RABIU MOHAMMED(LL.B)

Dear M.D.,

I am a Barrister and a member of Nigerian Bar Association(NBA). Your contact reached me through a member of our diplomatic mission abroad who recommended your reputation to me. Hence, I made up my mind to introduce this business to you in confidence for the mutual benefit of both of us.

The sum of US$25M (Twenty-five Million United States Dollars was lodged into one of the leading private banks here in the Country by the late Head of State (Gen. Sani Abacha), this money was lodged in a defaced form and in vaults/boxes. The money was originally meant to be used for his political campaign to suceed himself in office as the civilian President. Because, I was his family Attorney as such he confided in me and intimated me to witness and document all the relevant papers relating to this bank account, all these documents are still intact with me only. Incidentally, on 8th of June, 1998, Gen. Abacha died of "Cadiac Arrest".

As a matter of fact, I have adequately agreed with some

of the key officers of the private Bank to negotiate with you a trustworthy person to provide an account where this money could be transfered to your Country through your bank account, because we cannot claim this money here in Nigeria. We have concluded arrangements with an offshore security company to move this money through diplomatic means to a country where it could be directly transfered to your nominated account, to ensure absolute safety and risk free transfer of the money. After a successful transfer, 30% will be for you for your assistance, 5% for general expenses, 65% for us.

You are required to send by e-mail immediately your tel/fax numbers and bank particulars where this money will be lodged and your personal contact address. Once you notify me your willingness by sending the above requirements, this transaction will be concluded within 21 working days.

Best regards.
RABIU MOHAMMED(LL.B)

FROM: HON. GEORGE SALABI (BA.LLB)

SUBJECT: LEGITIMATE ARRANGEMENT

Dear President/ Managing Director,

I am Barrister George Salabi of the above law firm and the legal adviser to Engineer Permit Singh, a national of Malaysia who used to be a contractor with (ANGLO GOLD MINES) Mafikeng. Gold Mining/ Exploration Corporation in South Africa hereinafter shall be referred to as my client.

On February 21, 2004 my client, his wife and their three children were involved in a car accident. All occupants of the vehicle unfortunately lost their lives. Since then I have made several personal inquiries from the embassy to locate any of my clients extended relatives, this has also proved unsuccessful.

After several unsuccessful attempts, I now decided to inform you, hence I contacted you. I have send you this letter to assist in repatriating the money left behind by my client before they get confiscated or declared unserviceable by the bank where this huge deposit were lodged, particularly the FNB Bank of South Africa, where the deceased had a SAFE ACCOUNT CONTENT valued at about US$20,500,000.00 (Twenty Million, Five Hundred Thousand United States Dollars only) has issued me a notice to provide the next of kin or have the CONSIGNMENT confiscated though there are persons of same as a nationals here in South Africa non of them is a direct relative with the deceased and no one had an idea of this deposit. Since I have been unsuccessful in locating the

relatives for over a period of YEARS, I seek your consent to present you as the next of kin to the deceased since the bank would not released the CONSIGNMENT to ANY local person here is South Africa, I shall revalidate and notarize all the necessary legal documents that WILL back up any claim that the bank may need, this is a 100% risk free transaction because the banker who is in charge of account section is involved.   I will let you know the benefiting conditions of your help/involvement in my next message when I receive your positive response. I guarantee you this will be executed under a legitimate arrangement that will protect you from any breach of the law.

Kindly call me on my phone number before sending any fax or email message for security reasons. I need your strong assurance and confidentiality.

God bless us.
Best
regard

I shall revalidate and notarize all the necessary legal documents that WILL back up any claim that the bank may need, this is a 100% risk free transaction because the banker who is in charge of account section is involved. I will let you know the benefiting conditions of your help/involvement in my next message when I receive your positive response. I guarantee you this will be executed under a legitimate arrangement that will protect you from any

breach of the law.

Kindly call me on my phone number before sending any fax or email message for security reasons. I need your strong assurance and confidentiality.

God bless

us. Best

regards

HON. GEORGE

SALABI

(BARRISTER)

Here's one from an alleged 25 year old lady in Kenya. A measly $8.5 million in this one. Very compelling indeed.

My Dearest,

Good day to you, I have decided to contact you after much thought considering the fact that we have not meet before, but because of the circumstance oblige me, I decided to contact you due to the urgency of my present situation here in the refugee camp, I am Miss Jenny Kipkalya Kones, 25yrs old female and I from Kenya here in Africa; my father was the former Kenyan road Minister. He and Assistant Minister of Home Affairs Lorna Laboso had been on board the Cessna

210, which was headed to Kericho and crashed in a remote area called Kajong'a, in western Kenya. The plane crashed on Tuesday 10th, June, 2008. After the death of my beloved father my wicked step mother along with my uncles team together and sold everything that my late father had and share the

money within themselves. Unfortunately to me I fined my father's briefcase and when I opened it I found a document, which my late father use to deposit the sum of Eight Million Five Hundred Thousand United State Dollars
($8.500.000.00) in International Micro De Finance Bank, here in Burkina Faso
West Africa with my name as next of skin, right now I am in Ouagadougou Capital of Burkina Faso to withdraw the money so that i can start a better life and also further my education.

But on my arrival to the Bank, the Bank foreign Operation Department Director whom I meet in person told me that my father instruction to their bank is that the fund would only be release to me when I am married or present a trustee/partner who will help me and invest the fund overseas after the transfer, and the bank ask me to go and look for a foreign partner, that was why I decided to contact you, which I believe that you are going to be honest and reliable person that will help me and stand as my trustee/partner, so that I
can present you to the Bank for the release and transfer of the inheritance fund into your bank account in your country, and It is my intention to compensate you with 40% of the total fund for your services and help and the balance shall be my

capital in your establishment. As soon as I receive your positive response showing your interest i will put things into action, in the light of the above, I shall appreciate an urgent message indicating your ability and willingness to handle this transaction, awaiting your urgent and positive response, Please do keep this only to your self, i beg you not to disclose it to any body till i come over because am afraid of my wicked stepmother, i will send you my picture in my next email, with due respect, i am pleading that you help me, i am giving all this detailed information with every transparency believing that you will have a clear picture of the base of help i need from you.

I hope to hear from you soon, May truth and love be the guiding word in my refuge,

Best regard, Yours Sincerely
Jenny Kipkalya Kones.

Bibliography of 419 the Cyberscam game

1. **Jamie Shea**, the Deputy Secretary General for Emerging Security Challenges. **Euronews Tv** channel (Land of cybercrime).
2. Wikipedia
3. http://www.nigeria-law.org/Criminal%20Code%20Act-Part%20VI%20%20to%20the%20end.htm
4. EFCC (*Economic and Financial Crime Commission*) http://www.efccnigeria.org/
5. **www.419scammersexposed.com**,
6. www.aa419.org and
7. www.Hoaxbuster.com
8. *http://www.wikihow.com/Trace-an-IP-Address,http://forums.whatismyipaddress.com/viewforum.php?f=7*
9. Western Union, Money Gram
10. Precious blood of Jesus Christ
11. http://www.straightshooter.net/help_for_fraud_victims.htm
12. http://www.met.police.uk/fraudalert/419.htm
13. Unversity of Buea.

www.ingramcontent.com/pod-product-compliance
Lightning Source LLC
Chambersburg PA
CBHW071423050326
40689CB00010B/1960